THE LEGACY OF
LEON TROTSKY

THE LEGACY OF
LEON TROTSKY

INTERNATIONAL BOLSHEVIK TENDENCY

 BOLSHEVIK PUBLICATIONS

First published 2015 by
Bolshevik Publications
BCM Box 4771, London WC1N 3XX

ISBN: 9798850610562

© International Bolshevik Tendency
www.bolshevik.org
ibt@bolshevik.org
Facebook: Bolsheviks
Twitter: @ibt1917
Instagram: @bolsheviks1917
YouTube: @ibt1917

Typeset and designed by voluntary labor

Cover image: *Kazimir Malevich "Suprematism no. 58—Yellow & Black"*

CONTENTS

INTRODUCTION

ON 21 AUGUST 1940, Leon Trotsky succumbed to a massive head injury inflicted by a Stalinist assassin in Coyoacán, Mexico. One of the greatest revolutionary leaders in the modern era, Trotsky had risen from obscurity and persecution as a member of the underground socialist movement in the Tsarist Empire (imprisoned, banished to Siberia and forced into exile) to the height of power in the fledgling Soviet republic (organizer of the October Revolution and architect of the Red Army), only to be marginalized and once again exiled as the Russian Revolution degenerated under the weight of social, economic and political forces he himself brilliantly analyzed and combated.

Trotsky resembles a figure from Greek tragedy—save for the magnitude and historical significance of the tragedy, whose consequences extended well beyond the personal life of a single man. World history does not turn on the actions of individuals, however great they may be—but the life of Leon Trotsky was a rare example of the personal intertwining with the world-historic. The stage on which this historical actor played his part was grand, and the strengths and weaknesses, the triumphs and the defeats, the achievements and the mistakes of the man were themselves of historic consequence precisely because they were bound up with the practical organizing—at the highest echelons—of humanity's torturous transition from capitalism to socialism.

The historical importance of Trotsky lies not only in his critical association with the world's first successful proletarian socialist revolution, but in the political and theoretical contributions he made both before and after the Bolsheviks took state power. With the exception of V.I. Lenin, his co-leader of the Russian Revolution, Trotsky was unparalleled as an expositor and innovator of Marxism following the death of Marx and Engels. The brilliance and power of those contributions are such that, today, many leftists whose reformist political practice is sharply at odds with the revolutionary perspective of Trotsky nevertheless pay tribute to the "Old Man" of the Fourth International by falsely claiming his mantle as their own.

Given the pivotal importance of his contributions and the misappropriation of his name and political heritage, it is instructive to revisit Trotsky's legacy on the 75th anniversary of his death.

PART 1 | THE LONG ROAD TO
REVOLUTION

MENSHEVISM & BOLSHEVISM IN THE RSDLP

MARXISM IN RUSSIA originated in the early 1880s with the Emancipation of Labor grouping centered on George Plekhanov, widely recognized as the "father" of Russian Marxism. Competing with Narodnism (populism), which was more widely embraced at the time, the Emancipation group was at first largely confined to small study circles, distributing propaganda to a thin layer of advanced workers. With a strike wave and consequent turn toward mass work leading to large-scale recruitment in the mid 1890s, the recognized leadership of the Emancipation group—which spearheaded the founding of the Russian Social Democratic Labor Party (RSDLP) in 1898—began to recruit a new generation of Marxists, including Lenin, Julius Martov and Lev Davidovich Bronstein, a young militant from Ukraine, who would later adopt the party name Trotsky. Confined to clandestine work due to state repression (its first congress was dispersed by the authorities), the RSDLP barely functioned as an organization. In 1900, the party newspaper, *Iskra*, was founded under the émigré editorship of Lenin, speaking with the authority of the main party leadership and designed to cohere and politically educate members throughout the Tsarist Empire.

The founding and expansion of the RSDLP in the late 1890s coincided with the growth of a trend within the Russian workers' movement dubbed Economism, which had loose connections with the "evolutionary" socialism espoused by Eduard Bernstein in Germany at the turn of the century. Economism saw the struggle for socialism and the development of socialist consciousness as growing out of workers' struggles for "bread and butter" reforms. In his 1902 pamphlet *What Is To Be Done?*, Lenin spoke on behalf of the Iskraists when he attacked the Economists for "striving to *degrade* social-democratic politics to the level of trade union politics! [e.g., forming unions, enacting labor legislation]." Instead, he argued that socialist consciousness did not organically (i.e., "spontaneously") emerge from the day-to-day experience of workers:

> "this consciousness [socialist] could only be brought to them from without. The history of all countries shows that the working class, exclusively by its own effort, is able to develop only trade union consciousness, i.e., it may itself realize the necessity of combining in unions, for fighting against the employers and for striving to compel the government to pass necessary labor legislation, etc."

While the "from without" formulation was somewhat open to misinterpretation and later used against him, Lenin's central point was that economic struggles on their own were insufficient to generate revolutionary socialist ("social democratic" in the terminology of the times) consciousness—this required the active intervention of a revolutionary party to elevate the political understanding of the participants in the class struggle. Far from representing an "elitist" deviation from mainstream Marxism, Lenin's view was shared by Trotsky and the other Marxist leaders, and was wholly in keeping with the ideological orthodoxy of the Second International, to which the RSDLP belonged (see *Lenin and the Vanguard Party*, bolshevik.org).

That orthodoxy also included the broad, inclusive organizational conception—articulated most clearly by Karl Kautsky, leading figure of the German Social Democratic Party (SPD)—known as the "party of the whole class":

> "In order that the working class may put forward all its strength in the struggle against capitalism it is necessary that in every country there exist vis à vis the bourgeois parties, only *one* socialist party, as there exists only *one* proletariat."

> —Quoted in *Ibid.*

While the Second International had been built upon the basis of a socialist program, and Marxism was embraced by most party members, the "one party—one class" conception meant that the goal was to encompass all major political tendencies of the workers' movement. Although petty-bourgeois reformism would thereby find a home within the party, it was viewed as a relic of the immaturity of the working class: as the class developed in size and organizational capacity, it was reasoned, the objective situation would tend to undermine non-revolutionary elements. Lenin's insistence on the centrality of the Marxist party, while containing within it the seeds of an eventual break with the "party of the whole class" model in favor of the "vanguard" conception, was at the time nothing more than the commonly held view of all Marxists.

The Second Congress of the RSDLP met in July-August 1903 (first in Brussels, then in London) to formalize the already-existing leadership of the *Iskra* editorial board (which included the "old" guard of Plekhanov, Pavel Axelrod, Vera Zasulich and Alexander Potresov, and the younger Lenin and Martov), adopt a formal political program and establish criteria for party membership. Besides the Iskraist majority, which represented two-thirds of the delegates, the Economists and the Bund (a semi-nationalist tendency claiming sole representation of Jewish workers in the Tsarist Empire) were also represented at the congress. The Second Congress would have a profound impact on the future of the RSDLP and, by extension, the fate of the Russian Revolution—and it was also the occasion of a grave political error by the young Trotsky, one which would lead him down the wrong path for more than a decade.

Although seemingly united going into the congress, the Iskraists quickly divided into two camps over the question of membership— Lenin's "hards" and Martov's "softs." In an attempt to exclude opportunist elements and overcome the loose study-circle nature of the RSDLP, Lenin had proposed a membership criterion that required "personal participation in one of the Party organizations," as opposed to Martov's more vaguely defined "rendering [the party] regular personal assistance under the direction of one of its organizations." While seemingly trivial in nature, the difference in formulation anticipated the later division between the vanguard party of professional revolutionaries and the all-encompassing reformist (i.e., social-democratic in the modern sense) party—though this embryonic division was very far from being fully developed or understood by either camp. As Lenin explained, his intention was merely "to distinguish those who only talk from those who do the work" ("Second Speech in the Discussion on the Party," August 1903).

Martov's motion passed, but since his bloc partners, the Economists and Bundists, subsequently walked out of the congress over other related organizational issues, Lenin's group was left with a majority and Martov's group with a minority—and the Russian words for "Majorityites" (Bolsheviks) and "Minorityites" (Mensheviks) stuck. Lenin proposed a reduced *Iskra* editorial board with a Bolshevik majority (himself and Plekhanov), as well as the Menshevik Martov. By excluding respected figures of the old guard (Axelrod, Zasulich and Potresov), Lenin offended many delegates, including Trotsky, who had a sentimental attachment to his political elders. In the aftermath of the congress, Plekhanov, who had voted for Lenin's membership proposal but shied from a definite split over what seemed like a purely organizational matter, reneged and re-established the old editorial board configuration. Lenin resigned in protest, went on to establish a separate Bolshevik-led organization (the Bureau of Majority Committees) with its own newspaper (*Vperyod*), and held rival congresses, thereby deepening the split between the Bolshevik and Menshevik wings of the RSDLP. Still operating within the "party of the whole class" framework, Lenin viewed the Mensheviks as a petty-bourgeois tendency that had emerged in backward and peasant-dominated Russia and accidentally found itself within a Marxist party.

By the time of the Second Congress, Trotsky had already spent years in the workers' movement, and had been arrested and exiled to Siberia. He wrote articles for *Iskra* and collaborated with its London-based editorial board. In the months leading up to the congress, Lenin had even tried to co-opt Trotsky onto the editorial board. But when presented with Lenin's proposal for a new editorial board at the congress, Trotsky launched an attack on Lenin, accusing him of "substitutionism":

"In the internal politics of the Party [Lenin's] methods lead, as we shall see below, to the Party organisation 'substituting' itself for the Party, the Central Committee substituting itself for the Party organisation, and finally the dictator substituting himself for the Central Committee."

—*"Our Political Tasks,"* 1904

Trotsky's harsh treatment of Lenin was essentially without foundation. By extrapolating to absurdity the logic of Lenin's professional (or "hard") conception of party membership, Trotsky unwittingly provided an argument, seized decades later, linking Leninism with its antithesis, Stalinism. In his autobiography, written years after having been won to Bolshevism, Trotsky explained the motivation for his earlier pro-Menshevik views:

"My break with Lenin occurred on what might be considered 'moral' or even personal grounds. But this was merely on the surface. At bottom, the separation was of a political nature and merely expressed itself in the realm of organization methods. I thought of myself as a centralist. But there is no doubt that at that time I did not fully realize what an intense and imperious centralism the revolutionary party would need to lead millions of people in a war against the old order."

—*My Life*, 1930

Aside from his brief (but important) tenure working closely with the Bolsheviks as chairman of the St. Petersburg Soviet during the 1905 Revolution (see below), Trotsky spent the decade-and-a-half between the Second Congress and the outbreak of the Russian Revolution as a largely ineffectual organizational force within the socialist movement, at times closely associated with the Mensheviks, at others attempting in vain to engineer unity between the two factions from the outside. In contrast, Lenin spent this period building the nucleus of a programmatically solid vanguard party that would prove indispensable when a revolutionary opportunity again arose, as Trotsky himself later acknowledged:

"I believed that the logic of the class struggle would compel both [Bolshevik and Menshevik] factions to pursue the same revolutionary line. The great historical significance of Lenin's policy was still unclear to me at that time, his policy of irreconcilable ideological demarcation and, when necessary, split, for the purpose of welding and tempering the core of the truly revolutionary party."

—The Permanent Revolution, 1931

Attempts to unify the Bolsheviks and Mensheviks were made both by figures within the Russian workers' movement and by leaders of the Second International throughout the entire pre-WWI period (even as late as July 1914). However, the point of no return came with the 1912 Prague Conference, at which Lenin definitively broke with the Mensheviks and declared the Bolsheviks to be *the* RSDLP (see "Leninism: 'Irreconcilable Ideological Demarcation,'" *1917* No.35).

Yet Trotsky continued to push for unity. In an attempt to reverse the results of the Prague Conference, he engineered the unprincipled "August Bloc," which combined politically heterogeneous elements— the ultralefts (*Vperyodists*) and the right wing of Russian social democracy (Mensheviks, Bundists)—around little more than opposition to the person of Lenin. When the Bolsheviks refused to participate in the meeting organized by Trotsky, and the *Vperyodists* walked out, the "unity" conference, now dominated by Mensheviks, took on a decidedly anti-Bolshevik tone.

He later considered this to be one of his biggest political mistakes:

"I participated actively in this bloc. In a certain sense I created it. Politically I differed with the Mensheviks on all fundamental questions. I also differed with the ultra-left Bolsheviks, the *Vperyodists*. In the general tendency of policies I stood far more closely to the Bolsheviks. But I was against the Leninist 'regime' because I had not yet learned to understand that in order to realize a revolutionary goal a firmly welded centralized party is necessary. And so I formed this episodic bloc consisting of heterogeneous elements which was directed against the proletarian wing of the party....

"Lenin subjected the August bloc to merciless criticism and the harshest blows fell to my lot. Lenin proved that inasmuch as I did not agree politically with either the Mensheviks or the *Vperyodists* my policy was adventurism. This was severe but it was true.

"...I was sick with the disease of conciliationism toward Menshevism and with a distrustful attitude toward Leninist centralism. Immediately after the August conference the bloc began to disintegrate into its component parts. Within a few months I was not only in principle but organizationally outside the bloc."

—"From a Scratch—To the Danger of Gangrene (Part 2)," *In Defense of Marxism*, 1940

For Lenin, the idea of "unity" for its own sake was meaningless at best, destructive at worst:

"There can be no unity, federal or other, with liberal-labor politicians, with disrupters of the working-class movement, with those who defy the will of the majority. There can and must be unity among all consistent Marxists, among all those who stand for the entire Marxist body and the uncurtailed slogans, independently of the liquidators and apart from them.

"Unity is a great thing and a great slogan. But what the workers' cause needs is the *unity of Marxists*, not unity between Marxists, and opponents and distorters of Marxism."

—"Unity," April 1914

Despite the split at Prague, Lenin continued to formally adhere to the "one class—one party" organizational framework of the Second International and therefore still portrayed the Russian Mensheviks as petty-bourgeois radicals alien to the workers' movement. His own vanguard party conception was not yet fully developed. Indeed, Lenin would significantly revise this understanding only *after* the outbreak of WWI and the consequent collapse of the Second International into social-chauvinism (i.e., nationalist support for imperialism).

Revolutionary Organization: the 'Party of a New Type'

When Lenin read in *Vorwärts* (the central organ of the German party) that the SPD's members of parliament had voted to grant the government war credits on 4 August 1914, he is reported to have considered the newspaper a forgery. The SPD was the flagship section of the International, and many of its leaders (e.g., Friedrich Ebert, Gustav Noske, Philipp Scheidemann) came from decidedly working-class backgrounds. But the betrayal was not an aberration, and was repeated in other sections of the Second International. Something had gone fundamentally wrong with the project. Lenin was forced to confront the contradictions in the organizational methods of the International's "one class—one party" conception. That "one party" now included the social chauvinists supporting their ruling classes in the imperialist war, with whom "unity" was impossible. He concluded that a "party of a new type" was needed, one that would be built on solidly revolutionary Marxist principles, independent of all other shades of working-class opinion, from the outright social-chauvinists (e.g., Ebert, Noske, Scheidemann) to the vacillating and "centrist" elements (e.g., Kautsky) that excused the behavior of the social-chauvinists and refused to definitively break with them:

"The crisis created by the great war has torn away all coverings, swept away all conventions, exposed an abscess that has long come to a head, and revealed opportunism in its true role of ally of the bourgeoisie. The complete organisational severance of this element from the workers' parties has become imperative.... The old theory that opportunism is a 'legitimate shade' in a single party that knows no 'extremes' has now turned into a tremendous deception of the workers and a tremendous hindrance to the working-class movement. Undisguised opportunism, which immediately repels the working masses, is not so frightful and injurious as this theory of the golden mean.... Kautsky, the most outstanding spokesman of this theory, and also the leading authority in the Second International, has shown himself a consummate hypocrite and a past master in the art of prostituting Marxism."

—"The Collapse of the Second International," May-June 1915

Lenin now argued for splitting the workers' movement into its component political parts (i.e., "complete organizational severance"), called for a new (Third) International and proposed generalizing the method of party-building pursued by the Bolsheviks in the pre-war period:

"The Russian Social-Democratic Labour Party has long parted company with its opportunists. Besides, the Russian opportunists have now become chauvinists. This only fortifies us in our opinion that a split with them is essential in the interests of socialism.... We are firmly convinced that, in the present state of affairs, a split with the opportunists and chauvinists is the prime duty of revolutionaries..."

"In our opinion, the Third International should be built upon that kind of revolutionary basis. To our Party, the question of the expediency of a break with the social chauvinists does not exist, it has been answered with finality. The only question that exists for our Party is whether this can be achieved on an international scale in the immediate future."

—*Socialism and War*, 1915

At the same time, Lenin was working on an analysis of imperialism that provided a sociological explanation of reformism and opportunism as tendencies organically *internal* to the workers' movement that would never mechanically wither away over time. Instead, a hardened labor bureaucracy had arisen, acting as "watchdogs of capitalism" and as a transmission belt for pro-capitalist ideology inside the workers' movement:

"Is there any connection between imperialism and the monstrous and disgusting victory opportunism (in the form of social chauvinism) has gained over the labour movement in Europe?

"This is the fundamental question of modern socialism. And having in our Party literature fully established, first, the imperialist character of our era and of the present war, and, second, the inseparable historical connection between social-chauvinism and opportunism, as well as the intrinsic similarity of their political ideology, we can and must proceed to analyse this fundamental question....

"...the *opportunists* (social chauvinists) are working hand in glove with the imperialist bourgeoisie *precisely* towards creating an imperialist Europe on the backs of Asia and Africa, and... objectively the *opportunists* are a section of the petty bourgeoisie and of a certain strata of the working class who *have been bribed* out of imperialist superprofits and converted to *watchdogs* of capitalism and *corruptors* of the labour movement. "Both in articles and in the resolutions of our Party, we have repeatedly pointed to this most profound connection, the economic connection, between the imperialist bourgeoisie and the opportunism which has triumphed (for long?) in the labour movement. And from this, incidentally, we concluded that a split with the social-chauvinists was inevitable....

"The bourgeoisie of an imperialist 'Great' Power *can economically* bribe the upper strata of 'its' workers by spending on this a hundred million or so francs a year, for its *super*profits most likely amount to about a thousand million. And how this little sop is divided among the labour ministers, 'labour representatives' (remember Engels's splendid analysis of the term), labour members of War Industries Committees, labour officials, workers belonging to the narrow craft unions, office employees, etc., etc., is a secondary question....

"Lucrative and soft jobs in the government or on the war industries committees, in parliament and on diverse committees, on the editorial staffs of 'respectable', legally published newspapers or on the management councils of no less respectable and 'bourgeois law-abiding' trade unions—this is the bait by which the imperialist bourgeoisie attracts and rewards the representatives and supporters of the 'bourgeois labour parties.'"

—"Imperialism and the Split in Socialism," 1916

Years later, after he had been won to Bolshevism, Trotsky summarized Lenin's analysis of the roots of social chauvinism:

"Most of the labor parties in the advanced capitalist countries turned out on the side of their respective bourgeoisies during the war. Lenin named this tendency as social chauvinism: socialism in words, chauvinism in deeds. The betrayal of internationalism did not fall from the skies but came as an inevitable continuation and development of the policies of reformist adaptation. 'The ideological-political content of opportunism and of social chauvinism is one and the same: class collaboration instead of class struggle, support of one's own government when it is in difficulties instead of utilizing these difficulties for the revolution."'

"The period of capitalist prosperity immediately prior to the last war—from 1909 to 1913—tied the upper layers of the proletariat very closely with imperialism. From the superprofits obtained by the imperialist bourgeoisie from colonies and from backward countries in general, juicy crumbs fell to the lot of the labor aristocracy and the labor bureaucracy. In consequence, their patriotism was dictated by direct self-interest in the policies of imperialism. During the war, which laid bare all social relations, 'the opportunists and chauvinists were invested with a gigantic power because of their alliance with the bourgeoisie, with the government and with the general staffs.'...

"The intermediate and perhaps the widest tendency in socialism is the so-called center (Kautsky et al.) who vacillated in peace time between reformism and Marxism and who, while continuing to cover themselves with broad pacifist phrases, became almost without exception the captives of social chauvinists. So far as the masses were concerned they were caught completely off guard and duped by their own apparatus, which had been created by them in the course of decades. After giving a sociological and political appraisal of the labor bureaucracy of the Second International, Lenin did not halt midway. 'Unity with opportunists is the alliance of workers with their own national bourgeoisie and signifies a split in the ranks of the international revolutionary working class.' Hence flows the conclusion that internationalists must break with the social chauvinists. 'It is impossible to fulfill the tasks of socialism at the present time, it is impossible to achieve a genuine international fusion of workers without decisively breaking with opportunism...' as well as with centrism, 'this bourgeois tendency in socialism.' The very name of the party must be changed. 'Isn't it better to cast aside the name of Social Democrats, which has been smeared and degraded, and to return to the old Marxist name of Communists?' It is time to break with the Second International and to build the Third."

—"Lenin on Imperialism," 1939

In the midst of the Russian Revolution of 1917, Trotsky joined the Bolshevik Party, quickly becoming one of its top leaders. Lenin is reputed to have said that since Trotsky's adherence, there had been "no better Bolshevik" than his erstwhile adversary who had once denounced him for "substitutionism." Lenin, Trotsky and the other leaders of the Bolshevik (Communist) Party of Russia played a decisive role in founding the Third International in Moscow in March 1919 as a major step forward in the project of breaking with the "bourgeois tendency in socialism."

A revolutionary party cannot emerge semi-spontaneously through an "objective process" of class struggle divorced of conscious revolutionary intervention. Rather, it can only be built through the political development of cadres and their active participation in the class struggle on a Marxist program. Integral to the cohering of a revolutionary vanguard and the expansion of its influence within the working class (ultimately, to include a majority of that class) is ruthless political combat against reformism and centrism. Lenin did exactly this during the period of 19031917, while Trotsky sought to conciliate these same elements. As one of Trotsky's later followers succinctly put it:

"Trotsky's greatest error, the error which Trotsky had to recognize and overcome before he could find his way to unity with Lenin, was his insistence that the Bolsheviks and the Mensheviks had to unite.... Lenin's policy was vindicated in life. Lenin built a party, something that [Rosa] Luxemburg was not able to do with all her great abilities and talents; something that Trotsky was not able to do precisely because of his wrong estimation of the Mensheviks."

—"On 'Unity with the Shachtmanites'," James P. Cannon,
SWP internal bulletin, August 1945

A party that represents the "unity of the Marxists" can only be constructed on the basis of a genuinely revolutionary political program. Paradoxically, in terms of political analysis of Russia in the period before the 1917 revolution, Trotsky did not lag behind the Bolsheviks but rather ran ahead of them.

Revolutionary Program: 1905 & Permanent Revolution

Tsarist Russia at the turn of the 20th century was a backward country in which the vast mass of the population was agrarian, employed in small-scale farming. While the abolition of serfdom in 1861 had liberated much of the rural population from servitude to the landowners, peasants were still obliged to reimburse their former landlords, and various forms of feudal surplus extraction remained. For many peasants this meant ruin, and they were forced to sell their land and relocate to urban areas, where they joined the ranks of the burgeoning industrial proletariat. Wages were low and work days long. Discipline on the shop floor was maintained by firings and physical beatings, strikes and unions were illegal, and union organizers were routinely jailed or exiled. The Tsarist Empire openly identified as an autocracy, and political dissent was tightly curtailed. In addition to naked class exploitation was the national oppression enshrined in the Tsar's "prison house of peoples"—over half the inhabitants were non-Russians (Poles, Finns, Ukrainians, Azeris, Armenians, Georgians, etc.).

While retaining elements of feudal society, Russia combined this backwardness with an exceptionally modern industrial sector, which was capable of producing a wide range of commodities and industrial products (e.g., textiles, railway locomotives, armaments) that competed with those of the more advanced Great Powers. In 1908, giant industrial enterprises (those employing above 1,000 workers each) accounted for over 40 percent of all Russian workers, and in the industrial districts of St. Petersburg and Moscow, those numbers rose to 44 and 57 percent respectively, much higher ratios than in the United States, Britain and Germany.

Tsarist Russia was thus a land of stark contradictions: it possessed one of the largest empires on Earth, while at the same time it was a semi-client of Europe's more industrialized imperialist powers. Trotsky describes the peculiarities of Russia's "combined and uneven" development in the opening chapter of his magisterial work, *The History of the Russian Revolution*:

> "The fundamental and most stable feature of Russian history is the slow tempo of her development, with the economic backwardness,

primitiveness of social forms and low level of culture resulting from it....

"A backward country assimilates the material and intellectual conquests of the advanced countries. But this does not mean that it follows them slavishly, reproduces all the stages of their past....

"The laws of history have nothing in common with a pedantic schematism. Unevenness, the most general law of the historic process, reveals itself most sharply and complexly in the destiny of the backward countries. Under the whip of external necessity their backward culture is compelled to make leaps. From the universal law of unevenness thus derives another law which, for the lack of a better name, we may call the law of *combined development*— by which we mean a drawing together of the different stages of the journey, a combining of the separate steps, an amalgam of archaic with more contemporary forms. Without this law, to be taken of course, in its whole material content, it is impossible to understand the history of Russia, and indeed of any country of the second, third or tenth cultural class....

"But it is just in the sphere of economy, as we have said, that the law of combined development most forcibly emerges. At the same time that peasant land-cultivation as a whole remained, right up to the revolution, at the level of the seventeenth century, Russian industry in its technique and capitalist structure stood at the level of the advanced countries, and in certain respects even outstripped them....

"The confluence of industrial with bank capital was also accomplished in Russia with a completeness you might not find in any other country. But the subjection of the industries to the banks meant, for the same reasons, their subjection to the western European money market. Heavy industry (metal, coal, oil) was almost wholly under the control of foreign finance capital, which had created for itself an auxiliary and intermediate system of banks in Russia. Light industry was following the same road. Foreigners owned in general about 40 per cent of all the stock capital of Russia, but in the leading branches of industry that percentage was still higher. We can say without exaggeration that the controlling shares of stock in the Russian banks, plants and factories were to be found abroad, the amount held in England, France and Belgium being almost double that in Germany."

—The History of the Russian Revolution, 1930

This fundamental feature of Russia's development led Trotsky to develop his theory of "permanent revolution" following the momentous events of 1905. It was this program that would eventually be put into practice by the Bolsheviks in October 1917.

The 1905 Revolution, which Trotsky later referred to as a "prologue" for February and October 1917, occurred after the military defeat of the Tsar's army at the hands of Japan. On 9 January 1905, hundreds of thousands gathered in St. Petersburg to demand an eight-hour workday. The regime responded by brutally shooting hundreds of protesters. This "Bloody Sunday" massacre set off a huge outburst of anger that resulted in peasant attacks on landowners, mutinies in the army and navy, general strikes, and an attempted armed uprising in Moscow.

The revolution gave rise to "soviets" (i.e., workers' councils), the most important of which was the St. Petersburg Soviet of Workers' Deputies, established in October 1905 as a coordinating body of the general strike. Thrown up more or less spontaneously, the soviets were popular organs embracing the entire spectrum of the working class, their politically heterogeneous nature resulting in a diversity of opinion on a wide variety of issues. They constituted the organizational form of an alternative workers' state power:

> "The Soviet organized the working masses, directed the political strikes and demonstrations, armed the workers, and protected the population against pogroms.... The name of 'workers' government' which the workers themselves on the one hand, and the reactionary press on the other, gave to the Soviet was an expression of the fact that the Soviet really was a workers' government in embryo.
>
> "... The Soviet was, from the start, the organization *of the proletariat*, and its aim was the struggle for revolutionary power."

—"Summing Up," in 1905, Trotsky (1907)

Shortly after Trotsky returned to Russia in October 1905, he was elected vice-chairman of the St. Petersburg Soviet and became its head in late November. The Bolsheviks' initial reluctance to participate in the soviets meant that they were dominated by the Mensheviks, with Trotsky being their most prominent spokesperson. However, the all-embracing character of the soviets and the upsurge of militant mass activity produced a powerful impulse toward cooperation among both Bolsheviks and Mensheviks, in some cases resulting in fusions at the local level.

In early December 1905, when the St. Petersburg Soviet repudiated responsibility for loans made to the Tsar's government, the regime responded by disbanding the Soviet and arresting its leadership. In October 1906, Trotsky was sentenced to a second exile in Siberia.

The Tsar managed to weather the revolutionary upsurge by combining repression with political concessions—a constitution was granted and parliamentary elections were held. Loans from foreign banks allowed the Tsar to remain financially independent of the parliament (the "Duma"), which was eventually dispersed.

In the aftermath of 1905, the leadership of the RSDLP fell into three camps: the Mensheviks, who believed that Russia needed to undergo a period of capitalist development; the Bolsheviks, who projected a "revolutionary-democratic dictatorship of the proletariat and peasantry"; and Trotsky, whose theory of "permanent revolution" held that a working-class revolution, supported by the peasants, was on the agenda.

The Mensheviks considered the Russian working class to be too small to take power, and regarded any attempt to do so as a colossal blunder. Instead, they envisaged a strategic alliance with (i.e., political subordination to) the liberal wing of the bourgeoisie as the first phase of a "two-stage" road to socialism:

> "For Plekhanov, Axelrod and the leaders of Menshevism in general, the sociological characterization of the revolution as bourgeois was valuable politically above all because in advance it prohibited provoking the bourgeoisie by the specter of socialism and 'repelling' it into the camp of reaction. 'The social relations of Russia have ripened only for the bourgeois revolution,' said the chief tactician of Menshevism, Axelrod, at the Unity Congress [1906].

'In the face of the universal deprivation of political rights in our country there cannot even be talk of a direct battle between the proletariat and other classes for political power... The proletariat is fighting for conditions of bourgeois development. The objective historical conditions make it the destiny of our proletariat to inescapably collaborate with the bourgeoisie in the struggle against the common enemy.' The content of the Russian revolution was therewith limited in advance to those transformations which are compatible with the interests and views of the liberal bourgeoisie."

—"Three Concepts of the Russian Revolution," Trotsky, 1940

Lenin's conception of "the revolutionary-democratic dictatorship of the proletariat and the peasantry" shared elements of Trotsky's theory of permanent revolution. Lenin observed that the Russian bourgeoisie, unlike the French bourgeoisie of 1789, lacked the revolutionary will to see things through to the end and therefore equivocated, temporized and sought to make alliances with elements of the aristocracy. Instead, the peasantry, in alliance with the workers, would have to play the decisive role in the revolutionary overthrow of Tsarism, which would open the road for rapid capitalist economic development and lay the foundation for a future socialist revolution:

"Marxists are absolutely convinced of the bourgeois character of the Russian revolution. What does that mean? It means that the democratic reforms in the political system and the social and economic reforms, which have become a necessity for Russia, do not in themselves imply the undermining of capitalism, the undermining of bourgeois rule; on the contrary, they will, for the first time, really clear the ground for a wide and rapid, European, and not Asiatic, development of capitalism; they will, for the first time, make it possible for the bourgeoisie to rule as a class....

"We must be perfectly certain in our minds as to what real social forces are opposed to 'tsarism' (which is a real force, perfectly intelligible to all) and are capable of gaining a 'decisive victor' over it. Such a force cannot be the big bourgeoisie, the landlords, the factory owners, 'society' which follows the lead of the

Osvobozhdentsi [the liberals]. We know that owing to their class position they are incapable of waging a decisive struggle against tsarism; they are too heavily fettered by private property, by capital and land to enter into a decisive struggle. They need tsarism with its bureaucratic, police and military forces for use against the proletariat and the peasantry too much to be able to strive for its destructions. No, the only force capable of gaining 'a decisive victory over tsarism,' is the people, i.e., the proletariat and the peasantry. 'A decisive victory of the revolution over tsarism' is the *revolutionary-democratic dictatorship of the proletariat and the peasantry."*

—*Two Tactics of Social Democracy in the Democratic Revolution*

Lenin's concept of the "democratic" rule of the revolutionary peasantry and working class was abstract, and its connection to international socialist revolution unclear. Yet, as Trotsky later observed:

"Lenin's conception represented an enormous step forward [in contradistinction to the Mensheviks] insofar as it proceeded not from constitutional reforms but from the agrarian overturn as the central task of the revolution and singled out the only realistic combination of social forces for its accomplishment. The weak point of Lenin's conception, however, was the internally contradictory idea of 'the democratic dictatorship of the proletariat and the peasantry.' Lenin himself underscored the fundamental limitation of this 'dictatorship' when he openly called it bourgeois. By this he meant to say that for the sake of preserving its alliance with the peasantry the proletariat would in the coming revolution have to forego the direct posing of the socialist tasks. But this would signify the renunciation by the proletariat of its own dictatorship."

—*"Three Concepts of the Russian Revolution"*

The program of permanent revolution projected that the working class, supported by the majority of the peasantry, would lead the struggle for democracy (i.e., smash the Tsarist autocracy and expropriate the large landowners), while also undertaking the first stages of socialist construction:

"The perspective of the permanent revolution may be summed up in these words: The complete victory of the democratic revolution in Russia is inconceivable otherwise than in the form of the dictatorship of the proletariat basing itself on the peasantry. The dictatorship of the proletariat, which will inescapably place on the order of the day not only democratic but also socialist tasks, will at the same time provide a mighty impulse to the international socialist revolution. Only the victory of the proletariat in the West will shield Russia from bourgeois restoration and secure for her the possibility of bringing the socialist construction to its conclusion."

—Ibid.

The validity of the core propositions of Trotsky's permanent revolution—that the Russian bourgeoisie was too weak to realize the democratic tasks; the peasantry was incapable of acting independently; and the overthrow of Tsarism led by the working class would represent the opening chapter in an international socialist revolution—"was not revealed in 1905 only because the revolution itself did not receive further development," i.e., the workers and peasant revolt was contained. The confirmation of permanent revolution came a dozen years later when the Bolshevik Party led the workers to power in the October Revolution of 1917.

Imperialism & Internationalism in WWI

Prior to the outbreak of WWI, the Second International had formally stood on the principles of internationalism and working-class solidarity. Its founding congress in Paris in 1889 proclaimed that war was a product of class society and that it would remain until socialism had replaced capitalism. The congress also called for abolishing standing armies and replacing them with popular militias of the armed people.

In 1907 the Second International passed the "Stuttgart Resolution on Militarism and the International Conflicts," drafted by Lenin and Rosa Luxemburg, a leading figure in the left wing of the German SPD, which proposed:

"In case war should break out anyway, it is their [i.e., the working class and socialists'] duty to intervene in favour of its speedy termination, and with all their powers to utilize the economic and political crisis created by the war to rouse the masses and thereby to hasten the downfall of capitalist rule."

The "Basel Manifesto," adopted by the Second International in 1912, reiterated this sentiment and condemned the idea that socialists in any future conflict would side with their own imperialist rulers:

"The [proletarians] consider it a crime to shoot each other down in the interest and for the profit of the capitalism, and for the sake of dynastic ambition and of diplomatic secret treaties."

On 25 July 1914, leaders of the SPD proclaimed:

"Comrades, we appeal to you to express at mass meetings without delay the German proletariat's firm determination to maintain peace.... The ruling classes who in time of peace gag you, despise you and exploit you, would misuse you as food for cannon. Everywhere there must sound in the ears of those in power: 'We will have no war! Down with war! Long live the international brotherhood of peoples!'"

—Quoted in *Lenin and the Vanguard Party*

Ten days later, on 4 August 1914, the parliamentary fractions of both the French and German sections of the International abandoned any pretense of working-class solidarity and voted for war credits, thereby endorsing the imperialist aims of their respective rulers. The French reformists depicted their support for the war as a "defense of the Republic" against German militarism, while their German counterparts argued that a military defeat for Germany would negate all the gains the socialist movement had won in the past (e.g., trade-union organizations, numerous party newspapers and publications, parliamentary representatives).

After escaping en route to exile in Siberia in January 1907, Trotsky had moved to Vienna. As a Russian émigré, he was forced to flee Vienna for neutral Switzerland when the Austro-Hungarian Empire went to war with Russia in August 1914. While in Switzerland he wrote *The War and the International* (1914):

"Capitalism has created the material conditions of a new Socialist economic system. Imperialism has led the capitalist nations into historic chaos. The War of 1914 shows the way out of this chaos by violently urging the proletariat on to the path of Revolution....

"In these historical circumstances the working class, the proletariat, can have no interest in defending the outlived and antiquated national 'fatherland,' which has become the main obstacle to economic development. The task of the proletariat is to create a far more powerful fatherland, with far greater power of resistance— *the republican United States of Europe* as the foundation of the United States of the World....

"The collapse of the Second International is a tragic fact, and it were blindness or cowardice to close one's eyes to it....

"This book was written in extreme haste, under conditions far from favourable to systematic work. A large part of it is devoted to the old International which has fallen. But the entire book, from the first to the last page, was written with the idea of the New International constantly in mind, the New International which must rise up out of the present world cataclysm, the International of the last conflict and the final victory."

Trotsky's views on the imperialist war were in line with Lenin's anti-imperialist position of "revolutionary defeatism." Beginning from the necessity to "convert the imperialist war into civil war," Lenin argued:

"Both the advocates of victory for their governments in the present war and the advocates of the slogan 'neither victory nor defeat', equally take the standpoint of social chauvinism. A revolutionary class cannot but wish for the defeat of its government in a reactionary war, cannot fail to see that its military reverses facilitate its overthrow. Only a bourgeois who believes that a war started by the governments must necessarily end as a war between governments and wants it to end as such, can regard as 'ridiculous' and 'absurd' the idea that the Socialists of all the belligerent countries should wish for the defeat of all 'their' governments and express this wish. On the contrary, it is precisely a statement of this kind that would conform to the cherished thoughts of every class-conscious worker, and would be in line with our activities towards converting the imperialist war into civil war.

"Undoubtedly, the serious anti-war agitation that is being conducted by a section of the British, German and Russian Socialists has 'weakened the military power' of the respective governments, but such agitation stands to the credit of the Socialists. Socialists must explain to the masses that they have no other road of salvation except the revolutionary overthrow of 'their' governments, and that advantage must be taken of these governments' embarrassments in the present war precisely for this purpose."

—*Socialism and War*, 1915

Lenin denounced social-chauvinist claims that any of the imperialist belligerents were engaged in a "war of defense." He also asserted that when colonies or semi-colonies were attacked by imperialist powers, Marxists stood for the defeat of imperialism and the military victory of the dependent country:

"For example, if tomorrow, Morocco were to declare war on France, or India on Britain, or Persia or China on Russia, and so on, these would be 'just', and 'defensive' wars, *irrespective* of who would be the first to attack; any socialist would wish the oppressed, dependent and unequal states victory over the oppressor, slaveholding and predatory 'Great' Powers."

—*Ibid*.

In September 1915, a small number of left-wing socialist leaders from across Europe meeting in Zimmerwald, Switzerland condemned the social chauvinism of the official leadership of the Second International and raised the banner of working-class internationalism. While refusing to endorse Lenin's position of revolutionary defeatism, the "Zimmerwald Manifesto" denounced the imperialist slaughter and the war aims of the belligerent powers, called for a "fight for a peace without annexations or war indemnities" and urged workers to lift up the banner of socialism and embark upon "irreconcilable working-class struggle."

The Manifesto reaffirmed the Marxist principle of internationalism, despite the fact that its signatories (who included Trotsky, Lenin, Martov and Axelrod) had important political differences on a variety of issues. Despite this, the Bolshevik delegation viewed the Zimmerwald movement as a significant step toward a new, revolutionary International.

Lenin's policy of revolutionary defense of colonies and semi-colonies against imperialism was subsequently codified by the Third (or Communist) International. The Second Congress of the "Comintern," in 1920, adopted Lenin's "Twenty-One Conditions" for admission, including the following:

> "Any party wishing to join the Third International must ruthlessly expose the colonial machinations of the imperialists of its 'own' country, must support—in deed, not merely in word— every colonial liberation movement, demand the expulsion of its compatriot imperialists from the colonies, inculcate in the hearts of the workers of its own country an attitude of true brotherhood with the working population of the colonies and the oppressed nations, and conduct systematic agitation among the armed forces against all oppression of the colonial peoples."
>
> —"Terms of Admission into Communist International",
> July 1920

Internationalism, anti-imperialism and the permanent revolution were the key programmatic elements that allowed the Bolshevik Party, under the leadership of Lenin and Trotsky, to guide the Russian working class to power in October 1917.

The Russian Revolution & Civil War

The October Revolution of 1917, the most important event in modern history, marked the first time the working class successfully overturned capitalism and established a state power designed to serve the interests of the exploited and oppressed. The key to that success was the intervention of a revolutionary party with the political capacity to win the backing of the vast majority of Russia's workers and poor peasants.

The October Revolution, much like the "dress rehearsal" of 1905, was conditioned by military defeats suffered by the Tsarist regime. During the first half of 1914, a million workers had participated in a series of illegal strikes. One of the factors propelling Russia into the war was the hope within the ruling class that the conflict would produce a surge of nationalism to unify the nation and quell working-class dissent. When war broke out, Russia did experience a huge wave of patriotic fervor, like all the other combatants. Much of the left succumbed and supported the war, while the more left-wing groups who opposed participation in the war from the beginning, particularly the Bolsheviks and Martov's Menshevik Internationalists, suffered a sharp drop in support. Many neighborhoods, trade-union branches and factory shop floors that had once been Bolshevik strongholds, now turned on them.

However, as the war dragged on, casualties mounted and the economy frayed, the mood changed. By 1917, 10 million of the 15 million soldiers in Russia's army had been captured, seriously wounded or killed. In the days following International Women's Day on 23 February 1917, demonstrators cried "Bread!" "Down with autocracy!" "Down with the war!" (see "Five Days," in *The History of the Russian Revolution*). When the Petrograd (St. Petersburg) police turned their guns on the protests, the workers responded by setting up soviets, modelled on those of 1905. When, on 26 February, the Tsar demanded that the Petrograd garrison crush the upsurge, the soldiers responded by refusing orders and joining the protesters. The Tsar was forced to abdicate, and his regime collapsed.

To fill the void, a Provisional Government composed of representatives of various capitalist parties and "moderate socialists" (i.e., pro-capitalist reformists) was hastily assembled. The existence of this bourgeois body side-by-side with the workers' soviets (a nascent alternative governmental structure) created an unstable situation of "dual power," as Trotsky explained in *The History of the Russian Revolution*:

> "The political mechanism of revolution consists of the transfer of power from one class to another. The forcible overturn is usually accomplished in a brief time. But no historic class lifts itself from a subject position to a position of rulership suddenly in one night, even though a night of revolution. It must already on the eve of the revolution have assumed a very independent attitude towards the official ruling class; moreover, it must have focused upon itself the hopes of intermediate classes and layers, dissatisfied with the existing state of affairs, but not capable

of playing an independent role. The historic preparation of a revolution brings about, in the pre-revolutionary period, a situation in which the class which is called to realise the new social system, although not yet master of the country, has actually concentrated in its hands a significant share of the state power, while the official apparatus of the government is still in the hands of the old lords. That is the initial dual power in every revolution.

"But that is not its only form. If the new class, placed in power by a revolution which it did not want, is in essence an already old, historically belated, class; if it was already worn out before it was officially crowned; if on coming to power it encounters an antagonist already sufficiently mature and reaching out its hand toward the helm of state; then instead of one unstable two-power equilibrium, the political revolution produces another, still less stable. To overcome the 'anarchy' of this twofold sovereignty becomes at every new step the task of the revolution—or the counter-revolution."

—"Dual Power," Chapter 11

The Provisional Government, although officially recognized by Russia's military allies, had little popular support. The soviets, which had substantial authority with the plebeian masses, lacked official status and were distrusted by the propertied elites. This contradiction was initially masked by the fact that the soviets were dominated by reformist left parties that pledged allegiance to, and participated in, the Provisional Government.

Operating within the framework of Lenin's "revolutionary-democratic dictatorship of the proletariat and peasantry" and anticipating that the overthrow of Tsarism would usher in a period of bourgeois-democratic rule, the Bolshevik Party was initially disoriented by the February Revolution. The all-Bolshevik Third RSDLP Congress in 1905 had claimed:

"Depending upon the alignment of forces and other factors which cannot be precisely defined in advance, *representatives of our party may be allowed to take part in the provisional revolutionary government* so as to conduct a relentless struggle against all counter-revolutionary attempts and to uphold the independent interests of the working class."

—Quoted in *Lenin and the Vanguard Party* (our italics)

Events in February 1917 convinced Lenin to adjust this perspective and declare that the working class had to take power, with the support of the poor peasantry. This meant embracing the political core of Trotsky's permanent revolution.

In early April 1917, shortly after returning from exile, Lenin presented "The Tasks of the Proletariat in the Present Revolution" (aka the "April Theses"), which was sharply critical of the policy pursued by the resident Bolshevik leadership of Joseph Stalin and Lev Kamenev. Their attitude had been to conditionally support the Provisional Government, as Stalin explained in March 1917:

"...the Provisional Government has in fact taken the role of fortifier of the conquests of the revolutionary people.... It is not to our advantage at present to force events, hastening the process of repelling the bourgeois layers, who will in the future inevitably withdraw from us. It is necessary for us to gain time by putting a brake on the splitting away of the middle-bourgeois layers...

"In so far as the Provisional Government fortifies the steps of the revolution, to that extent we must support it; but in so far as it is counter-revolutionary, support to the Provisional Government is not permissible."

—"The March 1917 Party Conference (Part 1)," quoted in
The Stalin School of Falsification, Trotsky

In stark contrast, Lenin's "April Theses" declared:

"No support for the Provisional Government; the utter falsity of all its promises should be made clear.... Exposure in place of the impermissible, illusion-breeding 'demand' that *this* government of capitalists, should *cease* to be an imperialist government....

"The masses must be made to see that the Soviets of Workers' Deputies are the *only possible* form of revolutionary government.... [W]e preach the necessity of transferring the entire state power to the Soviets of Workers' Deputies"

A few days later Lenin specifically repudiated the "revolutionary-democratic dictatorship of the proletariat and peasantry":

> "This formula is already antiquated. Events have moved it from the realm of formulas into the realm of reality, clothed it with flesh and bone, concretised it and *thereby* modified it....
>
> "The person who *now* speaks only of a 'revolutionary democratic dictatorship of the proletariat and the peasantry' is behind the times; consequently he has in effect *gone* over to the petty bourgeoisie against the proletarian class struggle; that person should be consigned to the archive of 'Bolshevik' pre-revolutionary antiques (it may be called the archive of 'old Bolsheviks')."
>
> —"Letters on Tactics"

Despite Lenin's enormous political authority, his policy was widely regarded as sectarian by most of the Bolshevik cadre. Only after several weeks of intense political struggle did Lenin manage to win a majority of delegates at a Bolshevik conference in late April. *This political reorientation was decisive in opening the path to victory in October.* While many important political problems had to be solved during the subsequent six months, the acceptance of the "April Theses" set the strategic course toward proletarian revolution.

The Provisional Government soon demonstrated that it could satisfy neither the demands of the workers and peasants, nor those of the big landowners and capitalists. Increasingly large sections of the population began to see that the "dual power" in Russian society would not last indefinitely. Sooner or later there would either be a hard shift to the right, likely resulting in a military dictatorship committed to crushing the soviets and rebellious workers' movement, or a decisive turn to the left to oust the Provisional Government and establish working-class rule. As the middle ground disappeared, the growing social polarization strengthened both the Bolsheviks and the militarist counterrevolutionaries.

Lenin's "April Theses" and the policy of implacable opposition to the Provisional Government signaled a political convergence between Trotsky and the Bolsheviks on the decisive questions. Upon his return to Russia in May, Trotsky worked closely with the Bolsheviks, while formally adhering to the Mezhrayontsi (Inter-Borough) organization in

Petrograd, a small RSDLP grouping which briefly occupied a middle position between the Mensheviks and Bolsheviks. Trotsky later explained that: "The sole consideration which delayed my formal entry into the party for three months was the desire to expedite the fusion of the best elements of the Mezhrayontsi organization, and of revolutionary internationalists in general, with the Bolsheviks" (*Lessons of October*, 1924). He succeeded in negotiating fusion in July 1917.

In June 1917, Alexander Kerensky, the "socialist" who headed the Provisional Government, launched a military offensive that, despite initial promise, soon turned into a huge defeat. This broke the back of residual pro-war sentiment and translated politically into a dramatic popular swing to the left, favoring the Bolsheviks.

In July, Petrograd was rocked by large-scale armed pro-Bolshevik demonstrations by sailors, soldiers and workers who wanted to immediately bring down the Provisional Government. The Bolsheviks, who had promoted leftist dissent, believed that an insurrection would be premature because outside the capital, and Moscow, the reformists who backed the Provisional Government retained mass support. An attempted seizure of power by the Bolsheviks could have very easily been isolated and ended in a bloody defeat.

With the insurgent Petrograd masses held in check, Kerensky lashed out at the left, outlawing the Bolshevik party and jailing Kamenev and Trotsky, while Lenin and his closest collaborator, Gregory Zinoviev, fled to Finland to avoid arrest. Kerensky appointed General Lavr Kornilov, a far-right monarchist, as Commander-in-Chief of the armed forces. When Kornilov returned the favor by almost immediately plotting to oust Kerensky, attempts were made to dismiss him. He responded by beginning to mobilize his troops to march on Petrograd to disperse the Provisional Government and crush the workers' movement.

The Bolsheviks, who still enjoyed massive popular support among workers as well as sailors and soldiers, proposed a military bloc with Kerensky against Kornilov. Kerensky was in no position to refuse, and agreed to release the jailed Bolsheviks. Kornilov's forces were met by Bolshevik agitators who persuaded many of them to abandon their mission, thus removing the threat. A few weeks later when it was revealed that Kerensky had been conspiring with Kornilov, support for the Provisional Government fell to a new low, thus setting the stage for the Bolsheviks to make their move.

The question of insurrection produced another major debate within the Bolshevik leadership. Between July and October the Bolsheviks had gained solid majorities in the soviets in Petrograd and Moscow, as well as other urban centers. While their support was rising across the country, they did not yet have a majority in most of the smaller cities, particularly in the non-Russian parts of the empire.

Lenin, who insisted that the opportunity would not last long, favored a policy of striking immediately. As in April, he was initially isolated and unable to win a majority for several weeks. On 10 October the party leadership voted in favor of insurrection, but two members of the Central Committee, Kamenev and Zinoviev, who disagreed with the decision, broke discipline and revealed the Bolshevik plans. Lenin denounced them as "strikebreakers of the revolution," and unsuccessfully demanded their expulsion from the party. Though the Bolshevik plan was now exposed, Kerensky was simply too weak to act upon the information.

Trotsky, once again chairman of the Petrograd Soviet, proposed that the uprising be set to coincide with the opening of the Second All-Russian Congress of Soviets, whose delegates could then legitimize the seizure of power. The Military Revolutionary Committee of the Petrograd Soviet, which was headed by Trotsky and charged with the defense of the capital against counterrevolution, was the mechanism for coordinating the seizure of power. It had a Bolshevik majority but also included 14 members of the Left Social Revolutionaries and four anarchists. When the Provisional Government ordered the Petrograd garrison to the front, the soldiers mutinied and declared loyalty to the Soviet. This gave the Military Revolutionary Committee *de facto* military control of the capital. As Trotsky noted in retrospect:

> "The moment when the regiments, upon the instructions of the Military Revolutionary Committee, refused to depart from the city, we had a victorious insurrection in the capital, only slightly screened at the top by the remnants of the bourgeois-democratic state forms. The insurrection of October 25 was

only supplementary in character."

—Lessons of October

After Kerensky closed the Bolshevik press on 24 October, the Military Revolutionary Committee immediately reopened it:

> "The seals were torn from the building, the moulds again poured, and the work went on. With a few hours' delay the newspaper suppressed by the government came out under protection of the troops of a committee which was itself liable to arrest. That was insurrection. That is how it developed."

— The History of the Russian Revolution

Within hours Petrograd was in the hands of soldiers and Red Guards (workers' militias) loyal to the Military Revolutionary Committee. On 25 October 1917, the Red Guards seized the Winter Palace, the seat of the Provisional Government, and swept away the remnants of bourgeois rule.

The next day the Second All-Russian Congress of Soviets endorsed the seizure of power, and appointed a new cabinet with Lenin as the Premier and Trotsky as Minister of Foreign Affairs. Lenin's address to the congress began: "We shall now proceed to construct the socialist order." The delegates of the right wing of the Social Revolutionaries (i.e., peasant radicals) and the more conservative elements among the Mensheviks walked out in protest, prompting Trotsky to observe that they were headed for the "dustbin of history." The Left Social Revolutionaries, who formed a coalition government with the Bolsheviks, and a handful of minor party delegates, remained. A new state—comprised of workers', soldiers' and peasants' soviets led by a Bolshevik majority and defended by the armed working class—was born: the dictatorship of the proletariat.

Upon taking power the Bolsheviks immediately issued several important decrees that helped consolidate the new regime. The "Decree on Establishment of the Workers' and Peasants' Government" formally put power in the hands of the soviets. The "Decree on Peace" proposed to immediately withdraw Russia from the war and called for a conference at which all belligerents would agree to a peace without annexations or indemnities. The "Decree on Land," based on the Left SRs' agrarian program, called for the expropriation of large landowners, the nobility and the church, and for their land to be distributed to the poor peasants (see "The Land Question in the Russian Revolution," bolshevik.org).

Kerensky, who had escaped before the capture of the Winter Palace, gathered the forces he could muster. Four days after the Bolshevik-led revolution, Kerensky's supporters, commanded by Cossack General Peter Krasnov, counterattacked. In Petrograd the Red Guards quickly repelled the insurgents, but in Moscow fighting continued for several days with a substantial number of casualties.

The capitalist press around the world denounced the Bolsheviks as bloodthirsty maniacs and violent enemies of civilization. In fact, after the Kerensky-Krasnov episode, there was very little violence. Indeed, the Bolsheviks were initially extremely conciliatory to their opponents. Following Krasnov's aborted assault he was released after promising not to take up arms against the new regime again—a promise he broke within weeks.

The Bolsheviks, who anticipated that the October Revolution would quickly be aided by revolutions throughout Europe, moved very cautiously against propertied interests (with the exception of the church, nobility and large landowners). The Soviet government had no intention of nationalizing most of the large capitalist enterprises immediately, and only did so in May 1918 as a defensive measure.

Europe's rulers were far less conciliatory. Winston Churchill, Britain's Minister of Munitions, bluntly declared: "The baby [i.e., Soviet Russia] must be strangled in its crib." Prime Minister David Lloyd George said:

> "The whole of Europe is filled with the spirit of revolution.... The greatest danger that I see in the present situation is that Germany may throw in her lot with Bolshevism.... Once that happens all eastern Europe will be swept into the orbit of the Bolshevik revolution.... Bolshevik imperialism does not merely menace the states on Russia's borders. It threatens the whole of Asia and is as near to America as it is to France."
>
> —"Fontainebleau Memorandum," 25 March 1919

In December 1917, barely a month after the revolution, the British and French governments had worked out a division of labor for organizing the counterrevolution: France was to be responsible for Ukraine, while

Britain looked after the Caucuses. In addition to providing munitions and political support, Britain, France, the United States, Canada, Australia, Italy, Japan and half a dozen other countries intervened militarily in Russia's civil war on the side of the counterrevolutionary Whites. In May 1918, some 50,000 Czech prisoners, spurred on by the Allied powers and the Whites, revolted and seized a large chunk of Central Siberia.

The German rulers, with whom Trotsky as Minister of Foreign Affairs met in early 1918 at Brest-Litovsk (in present-day Poland) to discuss peace terms, proved no less hostile. The Bolshevik leadership was seriously divided over the negotiations: a left wing, led by Nikolai Bukharin, rejected on principle any compromise with the imperialists; Lenin, fearing an imminent collapse of Russia's armed forces, favored immediate acceptance of German terms; and Trotsky proposed a policy of "no peace, no war" (i.e., neither pursue the war, nor sign a treaty). Trotsky mistakenly calculated that given the *de facto* cessation of hostilities, Germany would not seek to grab more Soviet territory. When the German army began driving deeper into Russia, the Bolsheviks were forced to sign a humiliating treaty in which they gave up a third of the country and much of its industrial and agricultural capacity.

These concessions enraged the Left SRs, who quit the government and insurrected. They bombed the Bolshevik Central Committee building, killing 14 people; captured Felix Dzerzhinsky, the head of the Cheka (state security service); seized the Moscow telegraph center; assassinated the German ambassador; and shot Lenin (who survived but was seriously wounded). The Bolsheviks responded by banning the Left SRs. During the Civil War (1918-1921), the Bolsheviks resorted to "Red Terror" in defense of the Soviet regime (see "Conversation with an Anarchist," bolshevik.org), seeing these measures as temporary expedients necessitated by an acute danger.

The October Revolution of 1917 posed the gravest threat ever faced by global capitalism. By expropriating the ruling class and creating a new state power—a workers' government—Russia's insurgent proletariat sent shock waves around the world. The leadership provided by the Bolsheviks, particularly Lenin and Trotsky (including in his role as head of the Red Army), proved to be the decisive factor in the survival of the revolution. But the isolation of the Soviet workers' state, which was neither inevitable nor anticipated by the Bolsheviks, exacted a heavy price, and provided the context for the crucial political struggle over the fate of the revolution encapsulated in the conflict between Trotsky and Stalin following Lenin's death in 1924.

STALINIST DEGENERATION:
'SOCIALISM IN ONE COUNTRY'

ISAAC DEUTSCHER, AUTHOR of the brilliant three-volume Trotsky biography—*The Prophet Armed* (1954), *The Prophet Unarmed* (1959) and *The Prophet Outcast* (1963)—describes the situation facing the Soviet leadership in 1921:

"The nation ruled by Lenin's party was in a state of near dissolution. The material foundations of its existence were shattered. It will be enough to recall that by the end of the civil war Russia's national income amounted to only one-third of her income in 1913, that industry produced less than one-fifth of the goods produced before the war, that the coal-miners turned out less than one-tenth and the iron foundries only one-fortieth of their normal output, that the railways were destroyed, that all stocks and reserves on which any economy depends for its work were utterly exhausted, that the exchange of goods between town and country had come to a standstill, that Russia's cities and towns had become so depopulated that in 1921 Moscow had only one-half and Petrograd one-third of its former inhabitants, and that the people of the two capitals had for many months lived on a food ration of two ounces of bread and a few frozen potatoes and had heated their dwellings with the wood of their furniture—and we shall obtain some idea of the condition in which the nation found itself in the fourth year of the revolution...."

"Seven years of world war, revolution, civil war, intervention, and war communism had wrought such changes in society that customary political notions, ideas, and slogans became almost meaningless. Russia's social structure had been not merely overturned; it was smashed and destroyed. The social classes which had so implacably and furiously wrestled with one another in the civil war were all, with the partial exception of the peasantry, either exhausted and prostrate or pulverized."

—*The Prophet Unarmed*

Years of war and revolution had decimated the Russian working class and those who survived were completely exhausted. Many of the best elements had either been killed in the civil war or absorbed into the Bolshevik party and the administrative apparatus of the Soviet state. The Bolsheviks were forced to resort to "War Communism" (1918–21), a regime that substituted administrative fiat for the extension of workers' control in the factories and enforced requisitions of grain from the peasantry to feed the urban centers and army. Viewed as a short-term expedient, War Communism enabled the Red Army to defeat the Whites and win the civil war, but it generated enormous new contradictions within the isolated workers' state.

As soon as the immediate threat of Tsarist restoration had passed, the *smychka* (alliance between the urban proletariat and the poor peasants) began to fray. The peasants were petty proprietors who had only supported the Bolsheviks because of their land policies and in the knowledge that the Whites would have restored the big landowners. But, as the situation stabilized, the peasants sought to escape state control and yearned for the opportunity to sell their products to the highest bidder on the open market.

In March 1921, the naval garrison of Kronstadt, which had been solidly pro-Bolshevik in 1917, mutinied, raising the demand for "soviets without Bolsheviks." The original working-class sailors of Kronstadt had been ground up in the civil war and their places taken by more backward elements of peasant origin. The Bolsheviks initially sought to defuse the situation, but when this failed they were left with no alternative but to put down the revolt, whose leadership had established connections with counterrevolutionary White generals (see "Kronstadt & Counterrevolution," bolshevik.org).

The rising social tensions created by the devastation of the civil war eventually found expression within the Bolshevik Party itself. At the Tenth Party Congress in March 1921, the "Workers' Opposition" demanded that control of industry be given to the trade unions. While blaming the party leadership for the desperate situation of the working class, the Workers' Opposition remained loyal to the Soviet state and actively participated in suppressing the Kronstadt mutiny. Nevertheless, the congress felt that a split in the party was a real possibility that, in turn, could open the door to counterrevolution. It therefore took the extraordinary decision to ban internal party factions, in what was viewed as a temporary measure.

The Bolshevik leadership, led by Lenin, was painfully aware of the growing bureaucratic deformation of the workers' state. The failure of the revolutionary post-war upsurges to achieve any lasting gains abroad that would ease the pressure on the fledgling Soviet state made it necessary to attempt to find some means of reviving the economy on the basis of the limited internal resources available. At the March 1921 congress the Bolsheviks abandoned War Communism in favor of the "New Economic Policy" (NEP), along the lines of proposals made earlier by Trotsky (who had also advocated increased central planning and industrialization). The NEP replaced the forced requisitions of grain with a tax in kind on propertied agricultural producers—a concession to the restive peasantry that was aimed at reviving production and jump-starting an economy that was near collapse after years of war and famine.

While the NEP succeeded in increasing production it also created a layer of rich peasants (*kulaks*) and petty capitalists ("Nepmen") in the countryside. This stratum provided fertile ground for the growth of conservative tendencies within society, the party and the state. Compounding the problem was the continued isolation of the Soviet Union and the political demoralization resulting from defeats and missed revolutionary opportunities abroad, including Germany in 1918-1919, Hungary in 1919, Italy in 1919-1920, Germany again in 1921 and both Bulgaria and Germany in 1923.

By 1923, the temporary expedients necessary to prevent a collapse of the workers' state (see "Platformism & Bolshevism," bolshevik.org) had not prevented a process of degeneration reflected in the high-handedness of the party and state bureaucracies, which had essentially fused. The bureaucracy was well represented in the upper echelons of the government—and personified by Joseph Stalin who, as General Secretary of the Communist Party, had consolidated his supremacy by placing apparatchiks loyal to him in positions of power. Politically, the Stalin faction was marked by a growing disdain for what remained of workers' democracy, as well as by a Great Russian chauvinist attitude toward the myriad minority nations found throughout the Soviet Union.

Lenin had suffered a stroke in 1922, but when he became aware of Stalin's actions he launched a behind-the-scenes struggle to remove the General Secretary from his post, turning to Trotsky for help (see *Lenin's Last Struggle* by Moshe Lewin). In March 1923, Lenin suffered another debilitating stroke that virtually incapacitated him until his death in January 1924. Trotsky lacked Lenin's tactical/organizational experience and was resented as a newcomer by a significant section of the party cadres. He was outmaneuvered by Stalin, who formed a bloc with Zinoviev and Kamenev, known as the "Triumvirate," to consolidate their leadership of the party.

As a coherent movement to reverse the bureaucratic degeneration of the Russian Revolution and restore the Soviet state as an organizing center for world revolution, "Trotskyism" really emerged in October 1923. This was marked by the "Declaration of 46," a letter signed by prominent cadres detailing criticisms of bureaucratization, economic mismanagement and the lack of internal democracy in the Communist Party of the Soviet Union (CPSU), similar to those Trotsky had leveled only a few weeks earlier.

Trotsky's "Left Opposition" largely consisted of pre-1917 Bolsheviks and veterans of the revolution and civil war. In contrast, the vast majority of the party membership was much less experienced and politically sophisticated with an inclination to go along with the leadership. This was increased with the "Lenin levy" of early 1924 in which 240,000 raw recruits were admitted to the party en masse.

The central party leadership under Stalin, Kamenev and Zinoviev, along with Stalin's ally Nikolai Bukharin who had swung from the left to the right wing of the party, painted Trotsky as a pessimist, hostile to the peasantry and willing to risk the survival of the Russian workers' state for the sake of foreign revolutionary adventures. Stalin counterposed a conservative perspective of setting aside the pursuit of world revolution in favor of building "socialism in one country."

This essentially nationalist project of creating a classless, socialist society in a single country represented a radical departure from Bolshevik tradition. Only six months before the new doctrine was proclaimed, in the first edition of his *Foundations of Leninism*, Stalin had argued exactly the *opposite* point of view, as Max Shachtman recounts:

> "Stalin himself, who first formulated the theory of national socialism, wrote in the first edition of his 'Problems of Leninism' [a.k.a., 'Foundations of Leninism," April 1924] that
>
>> 'the main task of socialism—the organization of socialist production—still remains ahead. Can this task be accomplished, can the final victory of socialism in one country be attained, without the joint efforts of the proletariat of several advanced countries? No, this is impossible ... For the final victory of socialism, for the organization of socialist construction, the efforts of one country, particularly of such a peasant country as Russia, are insufficient. For this the efforts of the proletarians of several advanced countries are necessary.'
>
> "It is only in the second edition of the same work, printed in the same year, that he turned this clear and definite conclusion inside out and presented the still cautious formula which has since been developed into an unrestrained nationalistic gospel: 'After the victorious proletariat of one country has consolidated its power and has won over the peasantry for itself, it can and must build up the socialist society.'"
>
> —"Genesis of Trotskyism," 1933

"Socialism in one country," the central doctrine of Stalinism, represented a wholesale rejection of the militant internationalism which defined Lenin's party. Initially advanced as a factional club with which to beat Trotsky, this new nationalist perspective corresponded to the political mood of the bureaucracy, which was in turn reinforced by the weariness of the Soviet population. The theory, which was motivated by a desire to maintain the material basis of the bureaucracy, served to justify conservative domestic and foreign policies, and ultimately resulted in the destruction of the Third International as a revolutionary instrument.

In 1926, Stalin attempted to rationalize his volte-face as follows:

> "What is meant by the *possibility* of the victory of socialism in one country?
>
> "It means the possibility of solving the contradictions between the proletariat and the peasantry by means of the internal forces of our country, the possibility of the proletariat seizing power and using that power to build a complete socialist society in our country, with the sympathy and the support of the proletarians of other countries, but without the preliminary victory of the proletarian revolution in other countries.
>
> "Without such a possibility, building socialism is building without prospects, building without being sure that socialism will be completely built. It is no use engaging in building socialism without being sure that we can build it completely, without being sure that the technical backwardness of our country is not an insuperable obstacle to the building of a complete socialist society. To deny such a possibility means disbelief in the cause of building socialism, departure from Leninism."
>
> —*Concerning Questions of Leninism*, 1926

The issue of "socialism in one country" was not an arcane theoretical dispute—it had very significant political implications. Stalin's claim that the "final victory of socialism [in our country] is the full guarantee against attempts at [imperialist military] intervention" (*ibid.*) implied that one of the central responsibilities of revolutionaries abroad was to neutralize the imperialists and fight to maintain the global status quo. As Trotsky noted, this completely inverted the original *raison d'être* of the Communist International, which was established as an agency to promote revolutionary struggle:

"By the theory of national socialism, the Communist International is downgraded to an auxiliary weapon useful only for the struggle against military intervention. The present policy of the Comintern, its regime and the selection of its leading personnel correspond entirely to the role of an auxiliary unit which is not destined to solve independent tasks.

"The programme of the Comintern created by Bukharin is eclectic through and through. It makes the hopeless attempt to reconcile the theory of socialism in one country with Marxist internationalism, which is, however, inseparable from the permanent character of the world revolution. The struggle of the Communist Left Opposition for a correct policy and a healthy regime in the Communist International is inseparably bound up with the struggle for the Marxist programme. The question of the programme is in turn inseparable from the question of the two mutually exclusive theories: the theory of permanent revolution and the theory of socialism in one country. The problem of the permanent revolution has long ago outgrown the episodic differences of opinion between Lenin and Trotsky, which were completely exhausted by history. The struggle is between the basic ideas of Marx and Lenin on the one side and the eclecticism of the centrists [i.e., Stalinists] on the other."

—*The Permanent Revolution*, Trotsky

Trotsky and the Left Opposition pointed to the counterrevolutionary impact of the Stalin-Bukharin leadership's doctrine:

"The theory of socialism in one country inexorably leads to an underestimation of the difficulties which must be overcome and to an exaggeration of the achievements gained. One could not find a more anti-socialist and anti-revolutionary assertion than Stalin's statement [in 1926] to the effect that 'socialism has already been 90 percent realized in the USSR.' This statement seems to be especially meant for a smug bureaucrat. In this way one can hopelessly discredit the idea of a socialist society in the eyes of the toiling masses. The Soviet proletariat has achieved grandiose successes, if we take into consideration the conditions under which they have been attained and the low cultural level inherited from the past. But these achievements constitute an extremely small magnitude on the scales of the socialist ideal. Harsh truth and not sugary falsehood is needed to fortify the worker, the agricultural laborer, and the poor peasant, who see that in the eleventh year of the revolution, poverty, misery, unemployment, bread lines, illiteracy, homeless children, drunkenness, and prostitution have not abated around them. Instead of telling them fibs about having realized 90% socialism, we must say to them that our economic level, our social and cultural conditions, approximate today much closer to capitalism, and a backward and uncultured capitalism at that, than to socialism. We must tell them that we will enter on the path of real socialist construction only when the proletariat of the most advanced countries will have captured power; that it is necessary to work unremittingly for this, using both levers—the short lever of our internal economic efforts and the long lever of the international proletarian struggle."

—*The Third International After Lenin*, 1928

The most acute problem that this "short lever" was designed to address was what Trotsky termed a "scissors crisis," i.e., the growing disparity between rising prices for industrial goods and falling prices for agricultural products which threatened to pit urban workers against rural peasants and thereby destabilize the state. Trotsky and the Opposition proposed to address this by skimming off some of the social surplus produced by the peasantry and investing it in industrial production. This would expand the range and quality of manufactured products available while also increasing the social weight of the working class. While Bukharin invited the peasantry to "enrich yourselves!," the opposition warned of the dangers created by the emergence of a powerful layer of *kulaks* (wealthy peasants). As a counterweight the Opposition advocated the establishment of agricultural cooperatives and the granting of long-term credits to poorer peasants. The intent was to avoid the social polarization of rural society, and with it the growth of support for capitalist restoration, through promoting voluntary collectivization. The regime rejected these proposals, although several years later, when the kulaks attempted to apply pressure by cutting off food to the cities, Stalin reversed direction and implemented a brutal forced collectivization which set back Soviet agricultural production for decades.

Maximizing the power of the "short lever" also required reversing the bureaucratization of the Bolshevik Party and the Soviet state. The soviets had long been reduced to virtual rubber stamps for the directives of the party's executive committees and presidiums. Within the party itself, the selection processes, elections, internal political discussions and debates that had always characterized organizational life under Lenin were quickly disappearing. The Left Opposition raised the banner of returning to a "Leninist course" in their struggle to combat the bureaucratic strangulation of the Soviet workers' state and the party that had helped create it.

The Opposition sought to combat "officialism" (i.e., bureaucracy) by proposing to end the use of arbitrary appointments and dismissals of elected representatives; fostering workers' democracy in the trade unions and soviets; curbing the growing influence of the *kulaks*; and strengthening the *smychka* by drawing both workers and poor peasants into the administration of the state apparatus. They sought to revive "real inner-party democracy" by involving members in discussion and debate of current issues, including the publication of internal party bulletins; opening the party press to internal debates; a concerted bureaucratically expelled.

Although it failed to win mass support within the party's newly swollen ranks, the Left Opposition's defense of Leninist orthodoxy posed a potentially serious threat to the consolidation of the Stalinist bureaucracy. The Opposition was expelled in November 1927 but for many years continued to struggle under incredibly difficult conditions to uphold the essential elements of Leninism against the wholesale revision of Marxism that accompanied the bureaucratic degeneration of the Soviet workers' state.

The victory of Stalin's faction resulted in a qualitative transformation of the international Communist movement from an agency of world revolution to a tool of the Stalinist bureaucracy as it sought to strike deals with the imperialists. Over the course of the next decade, the Comintern was gradually turned into an agency for the realization of a consciously counterrevolutionary foreign policy. A major step in that process—and one that Trotsky fought—was the Kremlin's disastrous instructions to the fledgling Chinese Communist Party that resulted in the defeat of the second Chinese Revolution.

The Tragedy of the Chinese Revolution

By adopting Lenin's "April Theses" in 1917, the Bolshevik party had abandoned the "democratic dictatorship of the proletariat and the peasantry" in favor of a perspective that was functionally identical to that of Trotsky's permanent revolution. But no one, including Trotsky himself, had yet concluded that this experience would be applicable in colonial and semi-colonial countries where there had been no bourgeois-democratic revolution.

The early Communist International took great interest in attempting to forge close connections with anti-colonial movements. In stark contrast to the social chauvinism that characterized the Second International, the Second Congress of the Comintern in July 1920 clearly stipulated:

> "Any party wishing to join the Third International must ruthlessly expose the colonial machinations of the imperialists of its 'own' country, must support—in deed, not merely in word—every colonial liberation movement [and] demand the expulsion of its compatriot imperialists from the colonies...."
>
> —"Terms of Admission into Communist International"

The Comintern declared that communists had "the duty to support the revolutionary movement in the colonies," including bourgeois nationalist forces, while simultaneously promoting the "victory of soviet power." A resolution drafted by Lenin and approved by the Second Congress stated:

> "... the Communist International should support bourgeois-democratic national movements in colonial and backward countries only on condition that, in these countries, the elements of future proletarian parties, which will be communist not only in name, are brought together and trained to understand their

special tasks, i.e., those of the struggle against the bourgeois-democratic movements within their own nations. The Communist International must enter into a temporary alliance with bourgeois democracy in the colonial and backward countries, but should not merge with it, and should under all circumstances uphold the independence of the proletarian movement even if it is in its most embryonic form."

—"Theses on the National and Colonial Questions"

This somewhat algebraic formula left open the possibility of various forms of collaboration with bourgeois forces in colonial countries such as India or China. The "Theses on the Eastern Question" adopted by the Fourth Congress in 1922 advocated a strategy of seeking to establish "anti-imperialist united fronts" with "all revolutionary elements" in the colonial world, which hinted at a potential alliance with an "anti-imperialist" wing of the indigenous capitalist class.

The ambiguities in the early Communist International's attitude toward bourgeois-nationalist forces in the colonial world turned to tragedy in China in the mid-1920s where, under Stalin's leadership, the Comintern resurrected the Menshevik theory of "two-stage" revolution, i.e., political subordination to the bourgeoisie (see *The Tragedy of the Chinese Revolution* by Harold Isaacs).

In 1923, the Comintern had instructed the Chinese Communist Party (CCP) to fully enter the bourgeois-nationalist Kuomintang (KMT). Describing the KMT as a "workers' and peasants' party," the Kremlin sought to forge an "anti-imperialist united front" with General Chiang Kai-shek in pursuit of a "bloc of four classes" (i.e., workers, peasantry, urban petty bourgeoisie and the national bourgeoisie). To maintain such a bloc it was important to suppress any issues likely to alienate the "anti-imperialist" bourgeoisie. Inside the Kuomintang this translated into a policy of complete political subordination as CCP members were instructed not to criticize the utopian reformist doctrines of KMT founder Sun Yat-sen.

On 30 May 1925, the Shanghai municipal police fired on demonstrators and the labor movement, in which CCP members played a leading role, responded with a general strike that spread to Canton (present-day Guangzhou), Hong Kong and beyond. The strike wave alarmed the Kuomintang's bourgeois leaders and threatened the stability of the "anti-imperialist" alliance. Stalin signaled his desire to maintain friendly relations by accepting the Kuomintang as a "sympathizing" section of the Comintern in early 1926 and celebrating Chiang as an honorary member.

But Chiang was not mollified and in March 1926, as the strike continued, he raided strike headquarters, arrested CCP militants and removed communists from key posts within the KMT. The CCP leadership proposed to respond to Chiang's rightist coup by breaking with the Kuomintang, but Moscow insisted that the "anti-imperialist united front" be maintained. Stalin betrayed the Chinese communists by ordering a "compromise" with Chiang that involved providing the Kuomintang with a list of all CCP members as well as access to all Comintern-CCP communications.

In a speech in November 1926 Stalin invoked the formula of a "democratic dictatorship of the proletariat and the peasantry," explicitly rejected by Lenin in his April Theses, in order to defend his policy:

> "The point lies not only in the bourgeois-democratic character of [Chiang's] Canton government, which is the embryo of the future all-China revolutionary government; the point is above all that this government is, and cannot but be, an anti-imperialist government, that every advance it makes is a blow at world imperialism—and, consequently, a blow which benefits the world revolutionary movement....
> "I think that the future revolutionary government in China will in general resemble in character the government we used to talk about in our country in 1905, that is, something in the nature of a democratic dictatorship of the proletariat and the peasantry, with the difference, however, that it will be first and foremost an anti-imperialist government....
> "From this follows the task of the Chinese Communists as regards their attitude to the Kuomintang and to the future revolutionary government in China. It is said that the Chinese Communists should withdraw from the Kuomintang. That would be wrong,

comrades. The withdrawal of the Chinese Communists from the Kuomintang at the present time would be a profound mistake. The whole course, character and prospects of the Chinese revolution undoubtedly testify in favour of the Chinese Communists remaining in the Kuomintang and intensifying their work in it. "But can the Chinese Communist Party participate in the future revolutionary government? It not only can, but must do so. The course, character and prospects of the revolution in China are eloquent testimony in favour of the Chinese Communist Party taking part in the future revolutionary government of China. "Therein lies one of the essential guarantees of the establishment in fact of the hegemony of the Chinese proletariat."

— "The Prospects of the Revolution in China," 1926

A few months later in March 1927, as Chiang's army menaced the CCP stronghold of Shanghai, a demonstration of half a million workers turned into an insurrectionary general strike. Once again the Kremlin ordered the CCP not to break the "anti-imperialist united front" and demanded that the workers lay down their weapons, whereupon Chiang entered Shanghai, declared martial law and executed tens of thousands of leftists.

Incredibly, Stalin characterized Chiang's coup as a victory that would "strengthen and broaden the struggle against imperialism," claiming that the disaster in Shanghai heralded the beginning of a "second stage" of the revolution. Chinese communists were now instructed to rally to the "revolutionary" Left Kuomintang in Wuhan which had fallen out with Chiang:

"Chiang Kai-shek's coup signifies that the revolution has entered the second stage of its development, that a swing has begun away from the revolution of an all-national united front and towards a revolution of the vast masses of the workers and peasants, towards an agrarian revolution, which will strengthen and broaden the struggle against imperialism, against the gentry and the feudal landlords, and against the militarists and Chiang Kai-shek's counter-revolutionary group....

"It means that, by waging a resolute struggle against militarism and imperialism, the revolutionary Kuomintang in Wuhan will become in fact the organ of a revolutionary-democratic dictatorship of the proletariat and peasantry, while Chiang Kai-shek's counter-revolutionary group in Nanking, by severing itself from the workers and peasants and drawing closer to imperialism, will in the end share the fate of the militarists. "But it follows from this that the policy of preserving the unity of the Kuomintang, the policy of isolating the Rights within the Kuomintang and utilising them for the purposes of the revolution, no longer accords with the new tasks of the revolution. It must be replaced by a policy of resolutely expelling the Rights from the Kuomintang, a policy of resolutely fighting the Rights until they are completely eliminated politically, a policy of concentrating all power in the country in the hands of a revolutionary Kuomintang, a Kuomintang without its Right elements, a Kuomintang that is a bloc between the Kuomintang Lefts and the Communists."

—"Questions of the Chinese Revolution," 1927

But the "revolutionary Kuomintang" soon turned on its would-be allies in the CPP before itself being liquidated by Chiang's right-wing forces. By December 1927, with the disastrous consequences of the KMT orientation evident to all, Stalin executed an abrupt left turn and ordered the CCP in Canton to attempt an ill-advised and unprepared insurrection that was doomed to defeat. At one time hegemonic within China's small but combative working class, the CCP never recovered in the urban centers from the disaster of 1927, and instead, under Mao Zedong's leadership, took refuge in the countryside and pursued a strategy of peasant-based guerrilla warfare.

The question of China played an important role in the internal struggle within the CPSU after Lenin's death and factional calculations and miscalculations therefore influenced Trotsky's position at various points. The 1923 Opposition was more a collection of like-minded party members who agreed on several key issues rather than a cohered faction. While Trotsky was seen as the grouping's most authoritative figure, he maintained some public distance—with the 1921 ban on factions still in effect he was keen to avoid any questioning of his loyalty. The rapidly advancing bureaucratization of the party, manifested in part by the anti-"Trotskyite" witch-hunt of 1924, was alarming, but Trotsky remained the heroic founder of the Red Army and second only to Lenin in the eyes of the population. The post-war revolutionary tide was ebbing, and the Soviet Union was isolated for the time being, but the future course of events remained unclear. Lenin was ill and effectively sidelined, and Stalin had not yet emerged as an advocate of "socialism in one country." All of these factors contributed to the unwillingness of the 1923 Opposition to engage in hard factional warfare.

Stalin, whose organizational control of the central party administration permitted him to emerge as the leading figure in the CPSU, terminated the Triumvirate in 1925 and formed a bloc with Bukharin, the leader of the party's right wing. Zinoviev and Kamenev then gravitated toward Trotsky and his Left Opposition, and together they formed the Joint (or United) Opposition in mid-1926 just as events in China were unravelling. However, the United Opposition remained divided on the decisive questions of the Chinese Revolution.

As early as 1923, Trotsky had opposed the CCP's Kuomintang entry and his was the only dissenting vote when the issue arose in the Politburo. But Zinoviev, who had been chairman of the Comintern at the time and therefore shared responsibility for the entry, opposed the Joint Opposition calling for an exit from the KMT, and Trotsky felt compelled to concede:

> "In 1926 and 1927, I had uninterrupted conflicts with the Zinovievists on this question. Two or three times, the matter stood at the breaking point. Our center consisted of approximately equal numbers from both of the allied tendencies, for it was after all only a bloc. At the voting, the position of the 1923 Opposition [i.e., opposition to KMT entry] was betrayed by Radek, out of principle, and by Pyatakov, out of unprincipledness. Our faction (1923) was furious about it, demanded that Radek and Pyatakov be recalled from the center. But since it was a question of splitting with the Zinovievists, it was the general decision that I must submit publicly in this question

and acquaint the Opposition in writing with my standpoint....
"Now I can say with certainty that I made a mistake by submitting formally in this question."

—Letter to Max Shachtman, quoted in Shachtman's introduction to Trotsky's Problems of the Chinese Revolution

Trotsky made a similar compromise on the issue of permanent revolution and sought to downplay past differences with Lenin to undercut accusations of "Trotskyism." The September 1927 *Platform of the Joint Opposition* stated:

"We [Trotsky, Zinoviev and Kamenev] announced to the whole Communist International [15 December 1926]: 'It is not true that we are defending Trotskyism. Trotsky has stated to the International that in all those questions of principle upon which he disputed with Lenin, Lenin was right—and particularly upon the question of permanent revolution and the peasantry.' That announcement, made to the whole Communist International, the Stalin group refuses to print. It continues to accuse us of 'Trotskyism.'"

—Platform of the Joint Opposition

Trotsky's attempts to conciliate his bloc partners proved futile. Soon after the members of the Joint Opposition were expelled from the Communist Party, Zinoviev and Kamenev capitulated to Stalin in a vain attempt to regain their status in the party.

A long-time friend and loyal supporter, Adolph Joffe, in his last letter before committing suicide, astutely commented on Trotsky's tendency to seek a compromise in situations where it would have been better to have fought:

"I have never doubted the rightness of the road you pointed out, and as you know, I have gone with you for more than twenty years, since the days of 'permanent revolution'. But I have always believed that you lacked Lenin's unbending will, his unwillingness to yield, his readiness even to remain alone on the path that he thought right in the anticipation of a future majority, of a future recognition by everyone of the rightness of his path.

"Politically, you were always right, beginning with 1905, and I told you repeatedly that with my own ears I had heard Lenin admit that even in 1905, you, and not he, were right. One does not lie before his death, and now I repeat this again to you. But you have often abandoned your rightness for the sake of an overvalued agreement or compromise. This is a mistake. I repeat: politically you have always been right, and now more right than ever. Some day the party will realize it, and history will not fail to accord recognition. Then don't lose your courage if someone leaves you now, or if not as many come to you, and not as soon, as we all would like.

"You are right, but the guarantee of the victory of your rightness lies in nothing but the extreme unwillingness to yield, the strictest straightforwardness, the absolute rejection of all compromise; in this very thing lay the secret of Lenin's victories. Many a time I have wanted to tell you this, but only now have I brought myself to do so, as a last farewell."

—Letter to Trotsky, 16 November 1927

Joffe's admonition made a lasting impression on Trotsky and stiffened his resolve. He now drew the lesson of the Chinese tragedy and openly asserted the decisive importance of maintaining the complete political independence of the working class from all wings of the bourgeoisie. He clearly assigned responsibility for the debacle to Stalin and Bukharin:

"The Chinese Communist Party entered a bourgeois party, the Kuomintang, while the bourgeois character of this party was disguised by a charlatan philosophy about a 'workers' and peasants' party' and even about a party of 'four classes' (Stalin-Martynov). The proletariat was thus deprived of its own party at a most critical period.... The responsibility falls entirely on the ECCI and Stalin, its inspirers....

"*Never and under no circumstances may the party of the proletariat enter into a party of another class or merge with it organizationally.* An absolutely independent party of the proletariat is a first and decisive condition for communist politics."

—"The Political Situation in China and the Tasks of the Bolshevik-Leninist Opposition," *Writings of Leon Trotsky,* June 1929

Trotsky rejected any notion of a "democratic dictatorship" in favor of a strategy of permanent revolution (i.e., struggle for the dictatorship of the proletariat) as applicable not just to Russia, but to the entire semi-colonial and colonial world:

> "The 'democratic dictatorship' can only be the masked rule of the bourgeoisie during the revolution. This is taught us by the experience of our 'dual power' of 1917 as well as by the experience of the Kuomintang in China....
>
> "With regard to countries with a belated bourgeois development, especially the colonial and semi-colonial countries, the theory of the permanent revolution signifies that the complete and genuine solution of their tasks of achieving *democracy and national emancipation* is conceivable only through the dictatorship of the proletariat as the leader of the subjugated nation, above all of its peasant masses....
>
> "As all modern history attests—especially the Russian experience of the last twenty-five years—an insurmountable obstacle on the road to the creation of a peasants' party is the petty-bourgeoisie's lack of economic and political independence and its deep internal differentiation. By reason of this the upper sections of the petty bourgeoisie (of the peasantry) go along with the big bourgeoisie in all decisive cases, especially in war and in revolution; the lower sections go along with the proletariat; the intermediate section being thus compelled to choose between the two extreme poles. Between Kerenskyism and the Bolshevik power, between the Kuomintang and the dictatorship of the proletariat, there is not and cannot be any intermediate stage, that is, no democratic dictatorship of the workers and peasants."
>
> *—The Permanent Revolution*

Subsequent historical experience has vindicated Trotsky's analysis and repeatedly demonstrated that in countries with a "belated bourgeois development" (i.e., neocolonies) national independence from imperialist domination and agrarian revolution (distribution of land to the tillers) must be linked to the fight for workers' power. Revolutionary struggles of the oppressed must either culminate in the "dictatorship of the proletariat" or succumb to defeat.

But the Stalin-Bukharin bloc had effectively defeated Trotsky and the Left Opposition. In November 1927, Trotsky was expelled from the Russian Communist Party, a year later he was exiled from the Soviet Union and subsequently deprived of Soviet citizenship. Adherents of the Left Opposition in the USSR were subject to expulsion, forced confessions, exile, imprisonment and execution. Despite this, the Oppositionists maintained a perspective of fighting to reform and regenerate the Comintern and opposed the idea of building a new International. They maintained that the Comintern—which still commanded the allegiance of most revolutionaries in the international workers' movement—was the only home for genuine Bolshevik-Leninists because the process of degeneration that was destroying the communist movement and imperiling the Soviet Union was still reversible. It would take another massive defeat for the international working class—this time in Germany—for Trotsky and the International Left Opposition to conclude that the Third International, like the Second, belonged in the "dustbin of history."

The Rise of Fascism & Nazi Triumph in Germany

After his expulsion from the USSR, Trotsky lived on the Turkish island of Prinkipo (aka Büyükada). The capitulation by a number of prominent oppositionists (including Zinoviev, Kamenev, Karl Radek, Ivar Smilga and Evgeny Preobrazhensky) weighed heavily on him, as did his difficult financial and familial circumstances. Yet Trotsky closely followed political events in Russia and around the world, and was regularly visited by co-thinkers from Europe and elsewhere.

In the early 1930s Germany occupied a central place in international politics, as the ominous rise of Hitler's Nazi party threatened to plunge Europe into a new dark era. Trotsky's lucid analysis of fascism, contrasting with the confusionism of the Stalinist theoreticians, began with the observation that:

> "Fascism is not merely a system of reprisals, of brutal force, and of police terror. Fascism is a particular governmental system based on the uprooting of all elements of proletarian democracy

within bourgeois society. The task of fascism lies not only in destroying the Communist vanguard.... It is also necessary to smash all independent and voluntary organizations, to demolish all the defensive bulwarks of the proletariat, and to uproot whatever had been achieved during three-quarters of a century by the Social Democracy and the trade unions."

—"What Next?," 27 January 1932

Under the normal functioning of bourgeois democracy, capitalist rulers regard the fascist fringe as dangerous thugs. Yet in times of crisis, in the face of a combative workers' movement, the fascists have a certain utility for the propertied elites. In periods of social collapse fascist demagogues can gain a mass following among layers of the petty bourgeoisie (e.g., shop keepers, farmers, middle managers in the private sector and civil service) as well as among the chronically unemployed and impoverished underclass, and even some backward layers of the working class.

In Germany's 1928 election, Hitler's Nazis polled less than 3 percent, but as the economic conditions plummeted following the stock market crash of 1929, their vote shot up to 18 percent in 1930 and 37 percent in mid-1932. This gave the National Socialists a plurality of deputies in the German parliament, but the bourgeoisie was not prepared to turn over their state apparatus to the fascist rabble. When Hitler indicated a desire to become German Chancellor in 1932, head of state General Paul von Hindenburg scathingly responded: "That man for Chancellor? I'll make him my postmaster and he can lick stamps with my head on them" (*The Second World War*, Vol. 1, 1964, Winston S. Churchill). Between the July and November elections in 1932, the Nazi vote dropped by 2 million. Jospeh Goebbels, Nazi leader in Berlin, was devastated, writing in his diary: "The future looks dark and gloomy; all prospects and hopes have quite disappeared" (*The Rise and Fall of the Third Reich*, William L. Shirer and Ron Rosenbaum).

Two months later, however, Hitler ascended to the chancellorship unopposed. A critical reorientation had occurred within the upper echelons of the German ruling class which quickly swung momentum in favor of the fascists. In late January 1933, Kurt von Hammerstein, commander-in-chief of the Germany army and a known opponent of Hitler, drew the following conclusion:

"We [Hammerstein and outgoing-chancellor Kurt von Schleicher] were both convinced that only Hitler was possible as the future chancellor. Any other choice would lead to a general strike, if not civil war, and thus to a totally undesirable use of the army against the National Socialists."

—F.L. Carsten, *Reichswehr Politics*, 1973

A critical factor in the success of the Nazis was the deep division in Germany's powerful workers' movement between the German Communist Party (KPD) and the Social Democrats, whose combined support was potentially much larger than that of the fascists. Trotsky and the Left Opposition desperately called for united working-class action—a "workers' united front"—to crush the Nazi danger before it was too late. The Nazi brownshirts' success in attacking trade unionists, leftists, Jews and others they considered "undesirable" made them an attractive option for a ruling class concerned about the danger of a potentially insurgent workers' movement. Only by smashing the fascists on the streets could the danger posed by Hitler's movement be stopped, and that required concerted working-class mobilization. In 1933 Hitler himself observed:

"Only one thing could have broken our movement—if the adversary had understood its principle and from the first day had smashed, with the most extreme brutality, the nucleus of our movement."

—Quoted in "The Fight Against Fascism in the USA,"
SWP Education for Socialist Bulletins

Following the debacle in China and a revolt by the kulaks at home, Stalin had decreed a sharp left turn and announced that global capitalism had entered a new "Third Period" of terminal disintegration which would open the door to a series of revolutionary breakthroughs for the sections of the Comintern. Taking its cue from the Kremlin, the KPD projected the imminent collapse of German capitalism and its own rapid ascension to power. A key element of the new doctrine was the notion that social-democratic reformism (still embraced by the majority of the German working class) and fascism were "twins" and that the SPD was in fact a "social-fascist" organization ("socialist in words, fascist in deeds"). Instead of a united front with the SPD against the Nazis, the KPD called for rank-and-file social democrats to abandon their own organization and unite under KPD leadership in a "united front from below" (see "The Myth of the 'Third Period,'" *1917* No. 3, and "Not Twins, but Antipodes," 1917 No. 4).

Trotsky's call for a workers' united front was not an abstract call for unity, nor did it require a suspension of criticism. It was a specific proposal for joint action between the KPD and the Social Democratic Party (including its leadership), as well as other working-class organizations, to address the mortal danger posed by the rise of the Nazis:

"The front must now be directed against fascism. And this common front of direct struggle against fascism, embracing the entire proletariat, must be utilized in the struggle against the Social Democracy, directed as a flank attack, but no less effective for all that....

"It is necessary to show by deeds a complete readiness to make a bloc with the Social Democrats against the fascists in all cases in which they will accept a bloc. To say to the Social Democratic workers: 'Cast your leaders aside and join our "nonparty" united front' means to add just one more hollow phrase to a thousand others. We must understand how to tear the workers away from their leaders in reality. But reality today is the struggle against fascism. There are and doubtless will be Social Democratic workers who are prepared to fight hand in hand with the Communist workers against the fascists, regardless of the desires or even against the desires of the Social Democratic organizations. With such progressive elements it is obviously necessary to establish the closest possible contact. At the present time, however, they are not great in number. The German worker has been raised in the spirit of organization and of discipline. This has its strong as well as its weak sides. The overwhelming majority of the Social Democratic workers will fight against the fascists, but—for the present at least—only together with their organizations. This stage cannot be skipped. We must help the Social Democratic workers in action—in this new and extraordinary situation—to test the value of their organizations and leaders at this time, when it is a matter of life and death for the working class....

"Worker-Communists, you are hundreds of thousands, millions; you cannot leave for anyplace; there are not enough passports for you. Should fascism come to power, it will ride over your skulls and spines like a terrific tank. Your salvation lies in merciless struggle. And only a fighting unity with the Social Democratic workers can bring victory."

—Trotsky, "For a Workers' United front Against Fascism," December 1931

In September 1932, Ernst Thälmann, leader of the KPD, responded to the idea of a workers' united front:

"Trotsky gives one answer only, and it is this: the German Communist Party must join hands with the Social Democratic Party.... This, according to Trotsky, is the only way in which the German working class can save itself from fascism. Either, says he, the Communist party makes common cause with the Social Democrats, or the German working class is lost for ten or twenty years. This is the theory of an utterly bankrupt Fascist and counter-revolutionary.... Germany will of course not go fascist— our electoral victories are a guarantee of this."

—Cited in *The Prophet Outcast* (1963)

A decade earlier a document on the united front adopted by the Fourth Congress of the Comintern (drafted by Trotsky) had outlined precisely the approach the International Left Opposition proposed for the German workers' movement in the face of the Nazi threat:

"Does the united front extend only to the working masses or does it also include the opportunist leaders?

"The very posing of this question is a product of misunderstanding.

"If we were able simply to unite the working masses around our own banner or around our practical immediate slogans, and skip over reformist organizations, whether party or trade union, that would of course be the best thing in the world. But then the very question of the united front would not exist in its present form.

"The question arises from this, that certain very important sections of the working class belong to reformist organizations or support them. Their present experience is still insufficient to enable them to break with the reformist organizations and join us. It may be precisely after engaging in those mass activities, which are on the order of the day, that a major change will take place in this connection. That is just what we are striving for. But that is not how matters stand at present....

"The circumstances thus make wholly possible joint action on a whole number of vital issues between the workers united in these three respective organizations [i.e., communists, centrists and reformists] and the unorganized masses adhering to them.

"The Communists, as has been said, must not oppose such actions but on the contrary must also assume the initiative for them, precisely for the reason that the greater is the mass drawn into the movement, the higher its self-confidence rises, all the more self-confident will that mass movement be and all the more resolutely will it be capable of marching forward, however modest may be the initial slogans of struggle. And this means that the growth of the mass aspects of the movement tends to radicalize it, and creates much more favourable conditions for the slogans, methods of struggle, and, in general, the leading role of the Communist Party.

"The reformists dread the revolutionary potential of the mass movement; their beloved arena is the parliamentary tribune, the trade-union bureaux, the arbitration boards, the ministerial antechambers.

"On the contrary, we are, apart from all other considerations, interested in dragging the reformists from their asylums and placing them alongside ourselves before the eyes of the struggling masses. With a correct tactic we stand only to gain from this. A Communist who doubts or fears this resembles a swimmer who has approved the theses on the best method of swimming but dares not plunge into the water."

—"On the United Front," 1922, in *First Five Years of the*
Communist International

Had the KPD taken this approach in the early 1930s, the Social Democratic leaders would have been forced to choose between actively combating the fascists or exposing themselves to their ranks as unwilling to fight. Either way the KPD could have won the respect of militant social-democratic workers. And, most importantly, the fascist menace could have been crushed. Instead, the KPD's insistence that the SPD was itself a "social fascist" organization provided an alibi for the social democrats' reluctance to unite against the Nazis and thus helped pave the way for Hitler to come to power without any serious, organized opposition from the workers' movement. In short order both the KPD and SPD were destroyed.

Hitler's victory was a devastating defeat for the international working class. Up to that point, the International Left Opposition had sought readmission to the Communist International despite the disastrous policies pursued by the Kremlin, on the basis that the Comintern had not definitively demonstrated its historical bankruptcy. The absence of any significant opposition to the German disaster within the Stalinized Comintern now invalidated this perspective. On behalf of the leadership of the International Left Opposition, Trotsky thus raised the call for a new party in Germany and the building of a new International:

"From the day it was founded the Left Opposition has set itself the task of reforming the Comintern and regenerating the latter through Marxist criticism and internal faction work. In a whole number of countries, especially in Germany, the events of recent years have revealed with overwhelming force the fatal character of the policies of bureaucratic centrism [i.e., Stalinism]....

"Theoretically, the collapse of the German Communist Party still left two courses open to the Stalinist bureaucracy: either a complete review of the politics and the regime; or, on the contrary, a complete strangulation of all signs of life in the sections of the Comintern. The Left Opposition was guided by this theoretical possibility when, after advancing the slogan of a new

2: THE DEGENERATION OF THE RUSSIAN REVOLUTION | 65

party for Germany [in March 1933], it still left open the question of the fate of the Comintern....

"The Moscow leadership has not only proclaimed as infallible the policy which guaranteed victory to Hitler, but has also prohibited all discussion of what had occurred. And this shameful interdiction was not violated, nor overthrown. No national congresses; no international congress; no discussions at party meetings; no discussion in the press! An organization which was not roused by the thunder of fascism and which submits docilely to such outrageous acts of the bureaucracy demonstrates thereby that it is dead and that nothing can ever revive it. To say this openly and publicly is our direct duty toward the proletariat and its future. In all our subsequent work it is necessary to take as our point of departure the historical collapse of the official Communist International."

—"To Build Communist Parties and an International Anew,"
15 July 1933

PART 3 | BUILDING THE FOURTH
INTERNATIONAL

REGROUPMENT & ENTRISM

FOLLOWING THE DEBACLE of Third Period Stalinism in Germany, Trotsky recognized the necessity to launch a new International and sought to turn the Left Opposition outward, away from its previous orientation to the Comintern. After years as an external faction seeking to regenerate the CPSU and other sections of the International, in the summer of 1933 the Left Opposition changed its name to the International Communist League (ICL) and attempted to regroup with other leftist tendencies outside the Third International that identified with the Bolshevik tradition and began advocating for the creation of a new revolutionary leadership for the workers' movement:

> "[U]nder discussion now is not the immediate proclamation of new parties and of an independent international, but of preparing for them. The new perspective signifies first of all that talk of 'reform' and demands to restore oppositionists in the official parties must be put aside as utopian and reactionary.... The Left Opposition ceases completely to feel and act as an 'opposition.' It becomes an independent organization, clearing its own road. It not only builds its own fractions in the Social Democratic and Stalinist parties, but conducts independent work among nonparty and unorganized workers."
>
> —"To Build Communist Parties and an International Anew,"
> 15 July 1933

The ICL claimed the allegiance of some 4,000 to 5,000 militants spread across a dozen countries with a high proportion of intellectuals and few cadres with deep roots in the working class. It also lacked the resources for much of a full-time staff. In contrast, the Second and Third Internationals each had millions of adherents, significant bases in the labor movement, innumerable publications and powerful apparatuses.

Despite these shortcomings, the ICL's consistently revolutionary political line provided some important openings which were pursued with vigor:

"As early as June 15, 1933, that is, before the turn toward a New International, Trotsky addressed to the sections of the Left Opposition an article, *Left Socialist Organizations and Our Tasks*, in which he pointed out a new field of activity: The victory of German fascism had brought a crisis to the Social Democracy. The Comintern was losing its power of attraction. We could expect that the centrist organizations of the left would turn towards us. It was therefore necessary to turn our attention and our efforts in this direction.

"In fact, the whole political atmosphere, our orientation towards a new International, the arrival of Trotsky in France, actually attracted towards us the eyes of organizations which, in different periods and under different circumstances, had broken with the Second and Third Internationals. Numerous were the visits in Saint-Palais of leaders of these organizations (German S.A.P., English I.L.P., Dutch O.S.P. and R.S.P., etc.). The Dutch party of Sneevliet (R.S.P.) declared itself ready to join our ranks immediately."

—Jean van Heijenoort, "How the Fourth International was Conceived," 1944

The first step forward in the regroupment effort was the August 1933 signing of the "Declaration of Four: On the Necessity and Principles of a New International," which pledged to carry out "joint work for the regeneration of the revolutionary proletarian movement on an international scale." The three groups which co-signed this document with the ICL were the SAP (a left split from the German SPD in 1931) and two Dutch groups, the OSP (which broke from the social democrats in 1932) and the RSP (organized in 1929 by cadres expelled from the Dutch CP, led by veteran communist Henricus Sneevliet). The "Declaration of Four" outlined key programmatic points upon which a revolutionary party should be built: proletarian struggle for power culminating in the "dictatorship of the proletariat"; working-class internationalism and the repudiation of "socialism in one country"; revolutionary defense of the Soviet workers' state; internal party democracy and "democratic centralist" norms; and the need for a new Fourth International. In the end, the Trotskyists' insistence on programmatic clarity and revolutionary principle precluded unity with the other document signatories, whose conception of international organization tended toward a more federated, rather than democratic-centralist, model, which in turn led them to political oblivion within a few years.

In America the Trotskyists successfully seized the regroupment opportunities that presented themselves:

> "The American section [of the ICL] had decided early in 1934 that the way to apply the new 1933 [regroupment] orientation in the U.S. was to propose a fusion with the left centrist American Workers Party [AWP], headed by A.J. Muste.... There had been attempts in 1933 to fuse the German and Dutch sections with centrist groups in the London Bureau but they had fallen through. So the fusion of the American section with the AWP around a month after the October ICL meeting was the first time that this particular merger experiment was carried through. And it was a successful experiment, uniting the American cadre with an important group of effective mass workers and integrating most of them into the movement for the Fourth International."
> —George Breitman, "The Rocky Road to the Fourth International, 1933-1938"

The regroupments by the Trotskyists in the 1930s differ from recent "unity" campaigns by much of the contemporary far left because they were based on struggle for solid political agreement, not hasty paper unifications on the basis of a political lowest common denominator and an agreement to disagree (until the inevitable future split).

As the economic crisis of the 1930s propelled millions of workers and youth leftward, many joining the existing social-democratic parties, which in turn began to take on a more radical hue. In an attempt to intersect these elements, Trotsky advocated that his followers in France join the SFIO (French section of the Second International) whose leaders were in the process of establishing a common front with the Stalinist Communist Party. This tactical maneuver, known as the "French Turn," was also applied in other sections where the Trotskyists joined (or "entered") larger working-class political formations in order to win leftist elements within them to consistently revolutionary politics (see "The 'French Turn,'" *1917*, No.9). In *'Leftwing' Communism, An Infantile Disorder* (1920), Lenin had sketched out a similar tactic regarding the possibility of Third Internationalists in Britain affiliating to the Labour Party:

> "I cannot deal here with the second point of disagreement among the British Communists—the question of affiliation or non-affiliation to the Labour Party. I have too little material at my disposal on this question, which is highly complex.... it is beyond doubt that, in this question too, as always, the task consists in learning to apply the general and basic principles of communism to the specific relations between classes and parties, to the specific features in the objective development towards communism, which are different in each country and which we must be able to discover, study, and predict."

The argument for affiliation was that revolutionaries would be able to connect to the Labour ranks, and through their exemplary activity gradually win over the more leftist elements. Entry is a tactic that is really only useful in situations when there is major leftward movement within non-revolutionary organizations. It cannot become a long-term strategy without gutting it of any Leninist content in favor of a return to the Kautskyist notion of a "party of the whole class." As Trotsky observed: "Entry into a reformist centrist party in itself does not include a long perspective. It is only a stage which, under certain conditions, can be limited to an episode" ("Lessons of the SFIO Entry," *Writings of Leon Trotsky 1935-1936*, 30 December 1935).

French ICL members joined the SFIO in August 1934 in the midst of a working-class upsurge. The party's right wing had just walked out, and the leadership, moving sharply leftward, called on all revolutionaries to join the SFIO to fight for socialism. Within the SFIO the Trotskyists formed a faction, the Bolshevik-Leninist Group, which began publishing a newspaper, *La Vérité*. Despite complications throughout the entry due to internal differences, when the Trotskyists left the SFIO in early 1936 large numbers of Socialist youth came with them and the French section had more than tripled in size.

In the U.S., the Socialist Party (SP) was also growing quickly and most of its new recruits had illusions that it was a party for overturning capitalist rule. This led to a walkout by a section of its rightwing leadership at the end of 1935, pushing the party further to the left. The American Trotskyists were welcomed into the SP in 1936 with a couple of provisos— they had to close down their publications, *The Militant* and the *New International*, and they were not allowed to join as a group but only as individuals. Within the SP they quickly established good relations with many on the left wing, particularly among the youth. This alarmed the SP leadership who moved to expel the Trotskyists in late 1937. James P. Cannon, the historic leader of the SWP, summed up the results:

> "We accumulated invaluable political experience, and we more than doubled our forces as a result of the entry and one year's work in the Socialist Party....
>
> "Our entry into the Socialist Party had facilitated our trade union work. Our work in the maritime strike in California, for example, had been greatly aided by the fact that, at the time, we were members of the Socialist Party. Our comrades had better connections in the automobile workers union where, up to then, we had never had anything more than an occasional contact. The basis had been laid for a powerful fraction of Trotskyists in the automobile workers union....
>
> "We had won over to our side the majority of the Socialist youth and the majority of those Socialist workers really interested in the principles of Socialism and the Socialist revolution....
>
> "Partly as a result of our experience in the Socialist Party and our fight in there, the Socialist Party was put on the side lines.

This was a great achievement, because it was an obstacle in the path of building a revolutionary party. The problem is not merely one of building a revolutionary party, but of clearing obstacles from its path. Every other party is a rival. Every other party is an obstacle."

—James P. Cannon, *The History of American Trotskyism*, 1972

Programmatic firmness and tactical flexibility—hallmarks of the Bolshevik-Leninist tradition—were infused into the movement by Trotsky, often with great difficulty, in a period marked by historic upheavals and the rise of reaction but which also presented revolutionary opportunities.

Popular Frontism & the Spanish Civil War

The tumultuous years between Hitler's ascension to power in 1933 and Operation Barbarossa (the 1941 Nazi invasion of the USSR) saw wild oscillations in Soviet foreign policy—with the Comintern zigzagging along behind. Stalin, terrified by the rising power of fascist Germany, was anxious to forge "anti-fascist" alliances with capitalist "democracies," particularly Britain and France. The role of the Communist Parties outside the Soviet Union was to facilitate this diplomatic game by embracing "unity" with the "progressive" bourgeoisie. In both France and Spain in the mid 1930s the Communist Party deliberately squandered major revolutionary opportunities in pursuit of "popular front" (aka "peoples' front") electoral coalitions with their erstwhile "social fascist" social-democratic competitors as well as outright bourgeois parties. The liquidationist policy of the popular front produced results that were hardly less disastrous than the previous Third Period sectarianism.

In response to a leftist upsurge by Spanish workers after WWI, the bourgeoisie supported a 1923 radical rightist coup by General Primo de Rivera who ran a military dictatorship until he was ousted in January 1930. Popular opposition to monarchist-military rule forced the exile of King Alfonso XIII in April 1931, and led to the creation of a bourgeois republic headed by republican and "socialist" parties. In October 1934, a miners' strike in Asturias brought about an armed insurrection that resulted in a bloodbath, with 5,000 miners killed and some 30,000 taken prisoner. In the aftermath a political pact was made between the bourgeois republican parties and the Socialist Party (PSOE) known as the "Frente Popular" (Popular Front). In February 1936, the Frente Popular alliance won the general election on a platform that precluded any fight for workers' power in advance:

> "The republicans do not accept the principle of the national-ization of the land and its free reversion to the peasants.... The republican parties do not accept measures for nationalization of the banks...[and] workers control claimed by the delegation of the Socialist Party."
>
> —quoted in *The Stalin School of Falsification Revisited*,
> bolshevik.org

The Communist Party of Spain (PCE) had refused to support the first republican government in 1931, but with the abandonment of the "Third Period" and the new popular- front turn, the Spanish CP eagerly embraced the Frente Popular candidates in the February 1936 elections and instructed its elected members in the Cortes (parliament) to vote with the government.

The election of the Frente Popular in February 1936 panicked the Spanish ruling class, resulting in a rightist military revolt on 17 July 1936 led by General Francisco Franco. The Spanish working class responded immediately by organizing armed militias which routed the police and captured army garrisons in much of Spain. In Barcelona, Catalonia and Aragon insurgent workers and peasants took over the factories and landed estates abandoned by the wealthy elites.

This revolutionary upsurge alarmed Moscow as it threatened the entire international strategy of "unity" with the exploiters adopted at the Seventh Congress of the Communist International in August 1935, a policy that Comintern General Secretary Georgi Dimitrov specifically explained was counterposed to that of proletarian revolution:

> "Now the fascist counter-revolution is attacking bourgeois de-mocracy in an effort to establish the most barbarous regime of exploitation and suppression of the working masses. Now the working masses in a number of capitalist countries are faced with the necessity of making a *definite* choice, and of making

it today, not between proletarian dictatorship and bourgeois democracy, but between bourgeois democracy and fascism."

—"The Unity of the Working Class against Fascism,"
August 1935

When PSOE leader Largo Caballero took over as prime minister in September 1936 he brought two prominent representatives of the Spanish CP into his cabinet: Vincent Uribe as Minister of Agriculture and Jesus Hernández as Minister of Education. Hernández had clearly spelled out the PCE's opposition to any talk of social revolution a month earlier in the party newspaper *Mundo Obrero*:

"'It is absolutely false', declared Jesus Hernandez, editor of Mundo Obrero (August 6, 1936), 'that the present workers' movement has for its object the establishment of a proletarian dictatorship after the war has terminated. It cannot be said we have a social [i.e., revolutionary] motive for our participation in the war. We communists are the first to repudiate this supposition. We are motivated exclusively by a desire to defend the democratic republic.'

"*L'Humanité*, organ of the French Communist Party, early in August [1936] published the following statement:

'The Central Committee of the Communist Party of Spain requests us to inform the public, in reply to the fantastic and tendentious reports published by certain newspapers that the Spanish people are not striving for the establishment of the dictatorship of the proletariat, but know only one aim: the defence of the republican order, while respecting property.'"

—Quoted in Felix Morrow,
Revolution and Counter Revolution in Spain, 1938

In March 1937, José Diaz, the PCE General Secretary, addressing a plenary session of the PCE's Central Committee, explained why the party opposed the expropriations of the capitalists carried out by workers and peasants during the previous summer's revolutionary upsurge:

"[W]e should not lose our heads and skip over reality, trying to carry out experiments of 'Libertarian Communism' (Anarchist) or 'socialization' in the factories or in the countryside. The stage of the development of the democratic revolution through which we are passing requires the participation in the struggle of all anti-fascist forces, and these experiments can only result in driving away a very important section of those forces....

"If in the beginning the various premature attempts at 'socialization' and 'collectivization,' which were the result of an unclear understanding of the character of the present struggle, might have been justified by the fact that the big landlords and manufacturers had deserted their estates and factories and that it was necessary at all costs to continue production, now on the contrary they cannot be justified at all. At the present time, when there is a government of the Frente Popular, in which all the forces engaged in the fight against fascism are represented, such things are not only not desirable, but absolutely impermissible."

—*The Communist International*, May 1937, quoted in "Spain: War & Revolution," *1917* No.18

This spontaneous uprising of 1936 created an extremely unstable situation with many parallels to the "dual power" established in Russia in February 1917. The critical difference was that in Spain there was no sizeable revolutionary party capable of leading the spontaneous upsurge of the masses to victory.

The Communist Left of Spain (ICE), led by Andrés Nin, was one of the largest sections of the International Left Opposition in the early 1930s. In September 1935, Nin engineered a fusion between his group and Joaquín Maurín's Workers and Peasants' Bloc (BOC), adherents of Nikolai Bukharin's Right Opposition, to form the Partido Obrero de Unificación Marxista (POUM). Trotsky opposed the merger, arguing that the result was a group with a "centrist " (i.e., non-revolutionary) program." Trotsky severed relations with Nin when the POUM gave electoral support to the Frente Popular. In September 1936 the POUM entered the bourgeois government of Catalonia and Nin became Minister of Justice.

The break with the POUM reduced the number of Trotsky's adherents in Spain to a tiny handful who lacked the weight to play any significant role in subsequent events. Yet their program was powerfully vindicated when Trotsky's warnings of the terrible price the

Spanish workers' movement would have to pay for the POUM's class-collaborationist capitulation to popular frontism proved prescient.

When the Frente Popular electoral bloc was formed in January 1936, Trotsky immediately denounced the Socialist, Communist and anarcho-syndicalist signatories, but reserved his harshest criticism for the POUM: "The former Spanish 'Left Communists' have turned into a mere tail of the 'left' bourgeoisie. It is hard to conceive of a more ignominious downfall! ... [Their] conduct is nothing else than *betrayal of the proletariat for the sake of an alliance with the bourgeoisie.*" ("Treachery of the POUM," quoted in Leon Trotsky, *The Spanish Revolution* [1931-1939]).

Trotsky characterized popular frontism as the *"main question of proletarian class strategy"* and pointed to the historical parallel with the situation in Russia in 1917:

> "The question of questions at present is the People's Front. The left centrists seek to present this question as a tactical or even as a technical maneuver, so as to be able to peddle their wares in the shadow of the People's Front. In reality, the People's Front is the *main question of proletarian class strategy* for this epoch. It also offers the best criterion for the difference between Bolshevism and Menshevism. For it is often forgotten that the greatest historical example of the People's Front is the February 1917 revolution. From February to October, the Mensheviks and Social Revolutionaries, who represent a very good parallel to the 'Communists' [PCE] and Social Democrats [PSOE], were in the closest alliance and in a permanent coalition with the bourgeois party of the Cadets, together with whom they formed a series of coalition governments. Under the sign of this People's Front stood the whole mass of the people, including the workers', peasants', and soldiers' councils. To be sure, the Bolsheviks participated in the councils. But they did not make the slightest concession to the People's Front. Their demand was to break this People's Front, to destroy the alliance with the Cadets, and to create a genuine workers' and peasants' government.

> "All the People's Fronts in Europe are only a pale copy and often a caricature of the Russian People's Front of 1917, which could

after all lay claim to a much greater justification for its existence, for it was still a question of the struggle against czarism and the remnants of feudalism."

—Leon Trotsky, "The Dutch Section and the International," in *Writings of Leon Trotsky* (1935-36) [emphasis in original]

The Comintern's "new" popular- front orientation was simply a return to the discredited Menshevik strategy of two-stage revolution— i.e., building a broad cross-class alliance in defense of bourgeois democracy, and postponing the fight for socialism to the indefinite future. The corollary of this program is the necessity to respect bourgeois property:

"According to the Socialists and Stalinists, i.e., the Mensheviks of the first and second instances, the Spanish revolution was called upon to solve only its 'democratic' tasks, for which a united front with the 'democratic' bourgeoisie was indispensable. From this point of view, any and all attempts of the proletariat to go beyond the limits of bourgeois democracy are not only premature but also fatal....

"The Bolshevik point of view, clearly expressed only by the young section of the Fourth International, takes the theory of permanent revolution as its starting point, namely, that even purely democratic problems, like the liquidation of semi-feudal land ownership, cannot be solved without the conquest of power by the proletariat; but this in turn places the socialist revolution on the agenda. Moreover, during the very first stages of the revolution, the Spanish workers themselves posed in practice not merely democratic problems but also purely socialist ones. The demand not to transgress the bounds of bourgeois democracy signifies in practice not a defense of the democratic revolution but a repudiation of it."

—Trotsky, "The lessons of Spain: the last warning,"
17 December 1936

The Stalinists argued that a bloc with democratic elements among the Spanish capitalists was necessary for the immediate task of defeating Franco and winning the civil war. Rejecting Dimitrov's proposition that workers faced a "*definite* choice ... between bourgeois democracy and fascism," Trotsky returned to the Bolshevik experience:

> "Furthermore [argue the Stalinists], on the agenda stands not the revolution but the struggle against insurgent Franco.
>
> "Fascism, however, is not feudal but bourgeois reaction. A successful fight against bourgeois reaction can be waged only with the forces and methods of the proletariat revolution....
>
> "In the struggle against the socialist revolution [in 1917], the 'democratic' Kerensky at first sought support in the military dictatorship of Kornilov and later tried to enter Petrograd in the baggage train of the monarchist general Krasnov. On the other hand, the Bolsheviks were compelled, in order to carry the democratic revolution through to the end, to overthrow the government of 'democratic' charlatans and babblers. In the process they put an end thereby to every kind of attempt at military (or 'fascist') dictatorship."
>
> *—Ibid.*

Trotsky characterized the Spanish anarchists as having "no independent position of any kind in the Spanish revolution":

> "All they did was waver between Bolshevism and Menshevism. More precisely, the Anarchist workers instinctively yearned to enter the Bolshevik road (July 19, 1936, and May days of 1937) while their leaders, on the contrary, with all their might drove the masses into the camp of the Popular Front, i.e., of the bourgeois regime....
>
> "In and of itself, this self-justification that 'we did not seize power [in either July 1936 or May 1937] not because we were unable but because we did not wish to, because we were against every kind of dictatorship,' and the like, contains an irrevocable condemnation of anarchism as an utterly anti-revolutionary doctrine. To renounce the conquest of power is voluntarily to leave the power with those who wield it, the exploiters. The essence of every revolution consisted and consists in putting a new class in power, thus enabling it to realize its own program in life. It is impossible to wage war and to reject victory. It is impossible to lead the masses towards insurrection without preparing for the conquest power....

"In opposing the goal, the conquest of power, the Anarchists could not in the end fail to oppose the means, the revolution.... Thus anarchism, which wished merely to be anti-political, proved in reality to be anti-revolutionary and in the more critical moments—counter-revolutionary."

—*Ibid.*

As the bourgeois components of the Frente Popular gained strength they moved to reverse the gains that remained from the July 1936 uprising—taking land from the peasants, breaking up the militias and recreating a centralized military apparatus controlled by the Republican government. In 1937 the POUM was outlawed, and its leaders arrested. Nin was murdered in June by agents of Stalin's GPU. The shift to the right demoralized the workers and hastened Franco's victory.

The defeat of the Spanish Revolution, resulting from the pursuit of class-collaborationist policies, starkly vindicated the Bolshevik-Leninist program that was defended most eloquently and passionately by Trotsky:

"By way of compensation, a new generation of revolutionists is now being educated by the lessons of the defeats. This generation has verified in action the ignominious reputation of the Second International. It has plumbed the depths of the Third International's downfall. It has learned how to judge the Anarchists not by their words but by their deeds. It is a great inestimable school, paid for with the blood of countless fighters! The revolutionary cadres are now gathering only under the banner of the Fourth International. Born amid the roar of defeats, the Fourth International will lead the toilers to victory."

—*Ibid.*

Fourth International: Rearming the Leninist Vanguard

The founding of the Fourth International in September 1938 took place in the shadow of the sharpening inter-imperialist rivalries that erupted in World War II. The preceding five-year period, which Trotsky considered the "prehistory" of the International, had been rich with political lessons in the class struggle, as the Stalinist-led

Comintern stumbled from one disaster to the next. The insanity of the "Moscow Trials" (1936-1938), in which bizarre and grotesque allegations were levelled at party members, many of whom made false confessions before being summarily executed, discredited communism among many radicals who had previously been sympathetic to the Russian Revolution. Trotsky, who was convicted *in absentia* of heading a "Trotskyite-Zinovievite Terrorist Center" dedicated to killing Stalin and other Soviet leaders, spent much of a year organizing a campaign to expose the monstrous accusations. By the conclusion of the "Great Purge," only two of Lenin's "General Staff of 1917" (i.e., the Central Committee of the Bolshevik Party during the October Revolution) remained: Stalin and Trotsky. All the others who had not died of natural causes had been shot, committed suicide or "disappeared."

By 1938, the various centrist organizations with which the Trotskyists had earlier engaged with were well on the road to political oblivion. The three organizations which had co- signed the "Declaration of Four" in 1933 proclaiming the need for the Fourth International ended up in the centrist London Bureau (aka the "3½ International") along with the POUM, Britain's left-social democratic Independent Labour Party (ILP) and various others. The ICL's "entries" in the Socialist parties in France and the U.S., which had won important gains, had drawn to a close. With no other significant sources of recruitment open, and the dark shadow of impending world war deepening, Trotsky and his associates concluded that the time had come to found the Fourth International.

In March 1938, four leading members of the American Socialist Workers Party (SWP), James P. Cannon, Max Shachtman, V. R. Dunne and Rose Karsner, visited Trotsky in Mexico where he had been granted asylum. The SWP was the most significant section of the ICL so it was important for Trotsky to reach agreement with its leadership on the founding conference of the new international. During the meeting Cannon inquired:

> "'On the organizational side of the question—shall we consider this conference as a provisional gathering or as the actual founding of the Fourth International? The prevailing opinion among us is that we would actually form the Fourth International at this conference. We think that the main elements of the Fourth

International are now crystallized. We should put an end to our negotiations and maneuvers with the centrists and henceforth deal with them as separate and alien groupings.'

"Trotsky replied that he agreed 'absolutely' with what Cannon said.... 'Naturally we are a weak International,' he said, 'but we are an International.'"

—George Breitman, "The Rocky Road
to the Fourth International, 1933-1938"

Six months later the Fourth International was founded at a conference outside Paris, France. An SWP pamphlet on the event reported:

"[T]hirty delegates met ... on September 3, 1938, to found the Fourth International, to approve its program of action.... The delegates represented directly eleven countries: the United States, France, Great Britain (England and Scotland), Germany, the Soviet Union, Italy, Latin America [sic], Poland, Belgium, Holland and Greece....

"In addition to the organizations in these countries, there were quite a number of others which, for a variety of legal and physical reasons, were unable to send delegates but which are nevertheless wholeheartedly pledged to the Fourth International: Mexico, Cuba, Puerto Rico, Brazil, Colombia, Argentina, Uruguay, Peru, Chile, China, Indo-China, Union of South Africa, Australia, Spain, Norway, Austria, Czechoslovakia, Denmark, Canada, Switzerland, where sections exist, as well as small nuclei which, many of them for reasons of illegality, do not even have a regular press: Lithuania, Rumania, Yugoslavia, Bulgaria, New Zealand, Sweden, Ireland, Palestine, India, etc."

—"The Founding Conference of the Fourth International,"
1 January 1939

The "program of action" approved by the conference was Trotsky's *The Death Agony of Capitalism and the Tasks of the Fourth International* (aka the Transitional Program). Trotsky characterized its adoption as a "great achievement" and the movement's "most important conquest."

The central premises of the *Transitional Program* are clearly expressed in its opening lines:

"The world political situation as a whole is chiefly characterized by a historical crisis of the leadership of the proletariat. The economic prerequisite for the proletarian revolution has already in general achieved the highest point of fruition that can be reached under capitalism. Mankind's productive forces stagnate."

The advent of the imperialist epoch and the outbreak of the first global inter-imperialist conflict in 1914 marked the end of capitalism as a historically progressive mode of production. While this pointed to the *objective* need for working-class rule on the basis of socialized property forms, revolutionary Marxists reject the notion that capitalism must inevitably collapse. The central lesson of the Bolshevik Revolution is that a successful seizure of power by the working class requires the leadership of an organized revolutionary vanguard, composed of the most politically advanced elements of the class. The "crisis of leadership" Trotsky referred to was the absence of the *subjective* factor in the revolutionary equation: "The chief obstacle in the path of transforming the pre-revolutionary into a revolutionary state is the opportunist character of proletarian leadership; its petty bourgeois cowardice before the big bourgeoisie and its perfidious connection with it even in its death agony." The anarchists, social democrats and Stalinists had all revealed themselves as completely incapable of providing revolutionary leadership. Instead, Trotsky projected, "the wheel of history will demonstrate more clearly to the masses that the crisis of the proletarian leadership, having become the crisis in mankind's culture, can be resolved only by the Fourth International" (*Ibid.*).

The key problem is to bridge the gap between the objective need for social revolution and the political backwardness of the working class:

"It is necessary to help the masses in the process of the daily struggle to find the bridge between present demands and the socialist program of the revolution. This bridge should include a system of *transitional demands*, stemming from today's conditions and from today's consciousness of wide layers of the working class and unalterably leading to one final conclusion: the conquest of power by the proletariat...."

"The Fourth International does not discard the program of the old 'minimal' demands to the degree to which these have preserved at least part of their vital forcefulness. Indefatigably, it defends the democratic rights and social conquests of the workers. But it carries on this day-to-day work within the framework of the correct actual, that is, revolutionary perspective. Insofar as the old, partial 'minimal' demands of the masses clash with the destructive and degrading tendencies of decadent capitalism— and this occurs at each step—the Fourth International advances a system of *transitional demands*, the essence of which is contained in the fact that ever more openly and decisively they will be directed against the very bases of the bourgeois regime. The old 'minimal program' is superseded by the *transitional program*, the task of which lies in systematic mobilization of the masses for the proletarian revolution."

—*Ibid.*

The idea of transitional demands had already found explicit programmatic expression at the Fourth Congress of the Comintern in 1922 (see "Revolutionary Continuity and Transitional Demands," bolshevik,org/tp). Trotsky's contribution in drafting the *Transitional Program* was to codify the historical experience of the workers' movement, particularly the lessons of the October Revolution.

The mass homelessness and unemployment resulting from the economic crisis of the 1930s, were addressed in the *Transitional Program* by demands for decent housing for all and full employment through a "sliding scale of wages and hours":

"...the slogan of a *sliding scale of wages*.... means that collective agreements should assure an automatic rise in wages in relation to the increase in prices of consumer goods.

"...the slogan of a *sliding scale of working hours*.... [means] all the work on hand would then be divided among all existing workers in accordance with how the extent of the working week is defined. The average wage of every worker remains the same as it was under the old working week. Wages, under a strictly guaranteed *minimum*, would follow the movement of prices. It

is impossible to accept any other program for the present cata-
strophic period."

—*Transitional Program*

To complaints by the big capitalists that such demands are "unrealiz-
able," revolutionaries respond: "If capitalism is incapable of satisfying the
demands, inevitably arising from the calamities generated by itself,
then let it perish" (*Ibid.*). The program proclaims the necessity of fighting "uncompromisingly against any attempt to subordinate the unions
to the bourgeois state and bind the proletariat to 'compulsory arbitration' and every other form of police guardianship—not only fascist
but also 'democratic'." Successful defense of workers' interests requires
picket lines, "the basic nuclei of the proletarian army". "In connection
with every strike and street demonstration, it is imperative to propa-
gate the necessity of creating *workers' groups for self-defense*." In answer
to the deadly threat posed by scabs, fascists and cops, "It is necessary
to advance the slogan of a *workers' militia* as the one serious guarantee
for the inviolability of workers' organizations, meetings, and press."

Trotsky recalled the enormous role played in the Russian Revolution
by the emergence of soviets (aka workers' councils):

> "Soviets are not limited to an *a priori* party program. They throw
> open their doors to all the exploited. Through these doors pass
> representatives of all strata, drawn into the general current of
> the struggle. The organization, broadening out together with
> the movement, is renewed again and again in its womb. All
> political currents of the proletariat can struggle for leadership of
> the soviets on the basis of the widest democracy. The slogan of
> *soviets*, therefore, crowns the program of transitional demands.
> "Soviets can arise only at the time when the mass movement
> enters into an openly revolutionary stage. From the first mo-
> ment of their appearance, the soviets, acting as a pivot around
> which millions of toilers are united in their struggle against
> the exploiters[,] become competitors and opponents of local
> authorities and then of the central government. If the factory
> committee creates a dual power in the factory, then the soviets
> initiate a period of dual power in the country.

"Dual power in its turn is the culminating point of the transitional period. Two regimes, the bourgeois and the proletarian are irreconcilably opposed to each other. Conflict between them is inevitable. The fate of society depends on the outcome. Should the revolution be defeated—the fascist dictatorship of the bourgeoisie will follow. In case of victory—the power of the soviets, that is, the dictatorship of the proletariat and the socialist reconstruction of society, will arise."

—Ibid.

Much has changed since 1938, but the fundamental irrationality of global capitalism remains, as does the necessity for a profound reorganization of human society. The *Transitional Program* remains relevant today because it provides a guide to resolving the central problem facing humanity: the mobilization of the working class for state power.

Trotsky's Last Struggle: Defending the Gains of October

A year after the founding of the Fourth International, a serious political dispute erupted in its leading section that was to result in a deep split. Between August 1939 and April 1940, an internal factional dispute wracked the American SWP over the class nature of the USSR (often referred to as the "Russian Question"). Trotsky played a major part in what was to be his last political struggle. The vast majority of the Fourth International supported the SWP majority in asserting the Left Opposition's historic position that the Soviet Union was a degenerated workers' state that must be defended against capitalist attack. The SWP majority was led by James P. Cannon, who collaborated closely with Trotsky throughout the course of the factional struggle, documented in Cannon's *The Struggle for a Proletarian Party* (1940). The ICL had addressed the class nature of the Soviet Union in 1933, in the context of its shift from a policy of advocating political reform to outright political, as opposed to social, revolution aimed at removing the parasitic caste headed by Joseph Stalin:

" ... the privileges of the bureaucracy by themselves do not change the bases of the Soviet society, because the bureaucracy derives its privileges not from any special property relations peculiar to it as a 'class,' but from those property relations that have been created by the October Revolution and that are fundamentally adequate for the dictatorship of the proletariat.

"To put it plainly, insofar as the bureaucracy robs the people (and this is done in various ways by every bureaucracy), we have to deal not with *class exploitation*, in the scientific sense of the word, but with *social parasitism*, although on a very large scale...."

—"The Class Nature of the Soviet State," October 1933

Trotsky provided a fuller assessment of the character of the USSR a few years later in *The Revolution Betrayed* (1937):

"The Soviet Union is a contradictory society halfway between capitalism and socialism, in which: (a) the productive forces are still far from adequate to give the state property a socialist character; (b) the tendency toward primitive accumulation created by want breaks out through innumerable pores of the planned economy; (c) norms of distribution preserving a bourgeois character lie at the basis of a new differentiation of society; (d) the economic growth, while slowly bettering the situation of the toilers, promotes a swift formation of privileged strata; (e) exploiting the social antagonisms, a bureaucracy has converted itself into an uncontrolled caste alien to socialism; (f) the social revolution, betrayed by the ruling party, still exists in property relations and in the consciousness of the toiling masses; (g) a further development of the accumulating contradictions can as well lead to socialism as back to capitalism; (h) on the road to capitalism the counterrevolution would have to break the resistance of the workers; (i) on the road to socialism the workers would have to overthrow the bureaucracy. In the last analysis, the question will be decided by a struggle of living social forces, both on the national and the world arena."

A *political* revolution to overthrow the political monopoly of the Stalinist apparatus would leave intact the collectivized property relations, and in advocating it Trotsky maintained the position of "unconditional defense of the USSR" against capitalist restoration:

"What does 'unconditional' defense of the USSR mean? It means that we do not lay any conditions upon the bureaucracy.

It means that independently of the motive and causes of the war we defend the social basis of the USSR, if it is menaced by danger on the part of imperialism."

—"Again and Once More Again on the Nature of the USSR,"
In Defense of Marxism

The signing of the Stalin-Hitler Pact in August 1939, followed by Soviet occupation of eastern Poland and military intervention in Finland, outraged many European and North American left-liberals and radicals who had previously counted themselves among the "friends of the USSR." The wave of anti-Sovietism that accompanied the outbreak of World War II created pressure in the SWP to abandon the position of Soviet defensism. The oppositional minority, led by James Burnham, Max Shachtman and Martin Abern, did not agree among themselves —Burnham was rapidly breaking from any pretense of revolutionary politics, Abern claimed fundamental adherence to Trotsky's views while Shachtman occupied a shifting middle ground— but they all wanted to distance themselves from the SWP's historic position of Soviet defensism.

Burnham, the ideological leader of the minority, wrote:

"It is impossible to regard the Soviet Union as a workers' state in any sense whatever.... Soviet intervention (in the war) will be wholly subordinated to the general imperialist character of the conflict as a whole; and will be in no sense a defense of the remains of the Socialist economy."

—"On the Character of the War," 5 September 1939, cited in
Introduction to *In Defense of Marxism*

A month later Shachtman told an SWP plenum that the Soviet invasion of Poland was an "*imperialist policy*," and that what was required was a "revision of our previous concept of the 'unconditional defense of the Soviet Union'" (cited in *Ibid.*).

By April 1940, Shachtman and his followers, having split from the SWP to found the Workers Party, were advocating the defeat of "Stalinist imperialism":

"If, at a later stage, the present war between the imperialists should be transformed into an assault upon the Soviet Union, the slogan of defensism would have to be raised again, for it is not to the interests of the socialist world revolution and the working class to have one-sixth of the world, which the October uprising removed from the control of imperialism, restored to capitalist exploitation. In the present war, however, the world proletariat, the Russian included, cannot take upon itself a shadow of responsibility for the participation of the Stalinist bureaucracy in the imperialist conflict. The revolutionary vanguard must put forward the slogan of revolutionary defeatism in both imperialist camps...."

— "The Soviet Union and the World War,"
The New International, April 1940

The next year Shachtman reneged on his promise to defend the Soviet Union from imperialist assault. In 1941, when German imperialism invaded Russia, Shachtman argued: "There is therefore no place in this war for defense of the present Soviet régime under Stalin's dictatorship" ("The War in Russia," *The New International*, September 1941).

During the 1939-40 factional struggle, Trotsky drew a distinction between the revolutionary defense of the USSR by the Fourth International and that of the Stalinist policy "now being conducted under the slogan: 'For the Fatherland! For Stalin!'":

"*Our* defense of the USSR is carried on under the slogan: 'For Socialism! For the World Revolution! Against Stalin!' In order that these two varieties of 'defense of the USSR' do not become confused in the consciousness of the masses it is necessary to know clearly and precisely how to formulate slogans which correspond to the concrete situation....

"We must not lose sight for a single moment of the fact that the question of overthrowing the Soviet bureaucracy is for us subordinate to the question of preserving state property in the means of production of the USSR: that the question of preserving state property in the means of production in the USSR is subordinate for us to the question of the world proletarian revolution."

—"The USSR in War," *In Defense of Marxism*

The factional struggle in the SWP was conducted in accordance with the rules of Leninist democratic centralism. The minority was afforded every opportunity to air their views internally and the majority bent over backwards in an attempt to avoid a split.

When the minority did leave, they took out roughly 40 percent of the membership, including much of the youth and an important layer of journalists and talented intellectuals. In May 1940, only a month after leaving the SWP, Burnham renounced Marxism and the next year published *The Managerial Revolution* (1941), which impressionistically projected the Stalinist ruling caste, Germany's Nazi rulers and Roosevelt's New Dealers in the U.S. as "managerial bureaucracies" which were emerging as a new global ruling class. In the 1950s Burnham went on to be one of the original editors of William F. Buckley's ultra-conservative *National Review*. Shachtman ended up as a right-wing social-democratic Cold Warrior who infamously defended the CIA-led Bay of Pigs invasion in 1961. In 1962 he published *The Bureaucratic Revolution: The Rise of the Stalinist State*, in which he sought to prove that the USSR was a "new form of class society" he dubbed "bureaucratic collectivism." The political trajectory of the Shachtmanites graphically illustrated Trotsky's observation that revisionism on the "Russian question" could quickly progress "from a scratch to the danger of gangrene."

Postscript: Trotskyism after Trotsky

World War II, which devastated Europe and killed tens of millions, took its toll on the Fourth International. Many important cadres were murdered by fascists or Stalinists (including Trotsky himself) and those who survived were relatively inexperienced and easily politically disoriented by the dramatic changes in the global world order. The International was too shattered to take advantage of revolutionary opportunities thrown up in the immediate aftermath of the war. The leadership which did gradually emerge, under Michel Pablo, evolved into a revisionist current that sought to address what it took for a "New World Reality" by turning the Trotskyist movement into a left pressure group on Stalinists and Third World nationalists (see "Yugoslavia, East Europe and the Fourth International: The Evolution of Pabloist

Liquidationsim," "Genesis of Pabloism" (bolshevik.org) and "Revolution-ary Continuity & the Split in the Fourth International" (bolshevik.org/tp)).

The Fourth International split in 1951-53 with Cannon's SWP denouncing "Pabloist revisionism." A decade later the SWP reunited with the Pabloists over a shared uncritical enthusiasm for what they imagined to be the "unconscious Trotskyism" of Fidel Castro and the rest of the leadership of the Cuban Revolution (see "Cuba and Marxist Theory," bolshevik.org). The political forerunner of the International Bolshevik Tendency, the Revolutionary Tendency of the SWP, resisted this objectivist revisionism, and was expelled as a result.

Today, three quarters of a century after the assassination of Trotsky, many of his ostensible followers continue to search for short-cuts to success. In a constant search for "new" forms of political organization and strategy, they end up recycling the worn-out, discredited revisionism of the past.

Trotskyism is the revolutionary Marxism of our time—the political theory derived from over a century and a half of working-class expe-rience. Trotsky's legacy lives on in the struggle to reforge the Fourth International, world party of socialist revolution, as the indispensable lever in humanity's struggle to escape the irrational barbarism of capital-ism and lay the basis for the rationally planned, socialist world order of the future.

Printed in Great Britain
by Amazon

26238747R00056